So You Wanna Teach In
CHINA?

A Complete Resource Guide to Living and Teaching English in China

First Edition

JON DALLAS

pinkBLOT
PRESS

Copyright ©2016 by PinkBlot Press LLC. First Edition, 2016. All rights reserved. Printed in the United States of America. Except as permitted under Section 107 or 108 of the United States Copyright Act of 1976, no part of this book may be reproduced or transmitted in any form or by any means, electronic or mechanical, including photocopying, recording, scanning, or by any information storage and retrieval system, without written permission from the author, except for the inclusion of brief quotations in a review.

Requests to the Publisher for permission should be submitted online at http://www.pinkblotpress.com.

10 9 8 7 6 5 4 3 2 1

ISBN: 978-0-9862267-0-0 (book)

ISBN: 978-0-9862267-1-7 (ebook)

So You Wanna Teach In China?

is dedicated to the vast array of dedicated TESOL professionals committed to student centered educational leadership for the next generation of English speakers everywhere.

CONTENTS

About the Author ....*vi*

Acknowledgements ....*viii*

Introduction ....*x*

PART I: WORKING IN CHINA

Chapter One: English: The International Language 15

Chapter Two: China in a Nutshell 30

Chapter Three: Education in China 41

Chapter Four: The Chinese Visa Process 47

Chapter Five: Contracts 77

Chapter Six: Securing a Teaching Position 88

Chapter Seven: Retaining a Teaching Position 96

Chapter Eight: Classroom and TESOL Terminology..........104

PART II: LIVING IN CHINA

Chapter Nine: Technology and Telecom China's Big 3 111

Chapter Ten: Mainland Banking and Finance 115

Chapter Eleven: Housing 124

Chapter Twelve: Grocery Stores and Restaurants 133

Chapter Thirteen: APPs for Survival 139

Chapter Fourteen: Education Directors and Administrators...146

PART III: NETWORKING

Chapter Fifteen: Building a Professional Network 154

Appendix of Resources 168

Glossary..223

Bibliography..254

Index..258

About the Author

Jon Dallas is an American motivational speaker, author, and higher education professional with specialties in Teaching English to Speakers of Other Languages (TESOL), IELTS, TOEFL, SAT, study abroad, international student education, instruction, recruitment, and curriculum development. As an  accomplished educational leader, Mr. Dallas's continuous strategic vision is to bridge the classroom gap in global higher education between the United States of America, the People's Republic of China, and other South and Southeast Asian nations.

Mr. Dallas is currently Standardized Testing Consultant at Shenzhen's No.3 High School commissioned by the Shenzhen Education Bureau and the Ministry of Education of the People's Republic of China. He is former Senior Lecturer and Public Speaking Director at Yunnan Minzu University in Kunming, Yunnan where he instructs collegiate level courses in English Speech and Debate, Journal English, Survey of English Speaking Nations, Intermediate and Advanced Communication Principles, English Composition, Advanced Business English, International Business Negotiation, and International Trade Principles. Other seminars include Effective Public Speaking, TESOL

Teaching Approaches for Chinese Language Learners, Nonverbal Communication for Chinese Learners of English, and Cross Cultural Communication Principles.

Mr. Dallas's experience includes TESOL/TEFL/ESL, Chinese-American relations, international relations, international student enrollment, strategic sales techniques, relationship management, student relations with Southeast Asian nations, and public speaking. Since 2011, Mr. Dallas has refereed and coached dozens of students in preparation for the annual Foreign Language Teaching and Research Press (FLTRP) Cup English Public Speaking Contest (formerly the CCTV Cup English Public Speaking Contest) where contestants use their English public speaking abilities in a province-wide and national competition for top prizes and honors. As a native English speaker, Mr. Dallas commands varying proficiency in Mandarin, French and Spanish.

Mr. Dallas has instructed students from the United States, Canada, Mexico, India, Australia, the United Kingdom, Myanmar, Laos, Vietnam, Thailand, Cambodia, Malaysia, Indonesia, Taiwan, Hong Kong, mainland China's majority Han population, and over 25 ethnic minorities in mainland China. Mr. Dallas travels and works on several projects throughout China's Yunnan and Guangdong provinces.

Acknowledgements

I have not attempted to cite in the text all the authorities and sources consulted in the preparation of this manual. To do so would require more space than is available. The list would include departments of various governments, libraries, industrial institutions, periodicals and many individuals. Scores of people contributed to this book and to my sanity while writing this book. Information and illustrations have been contributed by Yunnan Minzu University, Yunnan Normal University, Yunnan University, Yunnan Agricultural University, Southwest Forestry University, Yunnan University of Finance and Economics, Shenzhen International Personnel Training Centre, EF English First, Gold Star TEFL Recruitment, University of Phoenix, NAFSA, The British Council, ESL International, ELT Professionals Around the World, Inside Higher Education, Confucius Institute, Friends of China, People's Republic of China Ministry of Education, American Chamber of Commerce in China, Rebekah McCormack, Eric Charles Jones, Dima M. Fayyad, Charles Anthony Hill, James L. Harrison, Roberta Boyle, Deborah West, Glynis Machaterre, Michael J. Dremel, Kevin M. Salcido, Yuan Yongzhen 林宏伟 (John Lin), Zhou Piao 周飘 (Chris Zhou), Pei Junyun 裴军运 (Jason Pei), Jiang Jinling 将金玲 (Jolin Jiang), Wang Wei 王伟 (Peter Wang), Ling Xiaofeng 凌晓凤 (Chrissy Ling), Zheng Wei 郑为, Yang Kaijun 杨开军 (Tony Yang), Wang Xiaolu 王小璐 (Jade "Caro" Wang), Lu Shihua 卢世华 (Stone Lu), Wu Jianghai 武江海, Yang Deng 杨邓, Zhao Weijie 赵韦杰, Li Xiaohua 李孝华 (Bill Lee), Han Jianhui 韩剑晖 (Ray Han), Qi Song 齐松 (William Qi), Qin Haonan 秦昊楠 (Charles Qin), Liu Xun 刘勋; Vice President/Professor Yuan Yichuan 原一川, Yunnan Normal University 云南师范大学; Dean/Professor Zi Gusheng 资谷生, Yunnan Agricultural University 云南农业大学; Dean/Professor Li Xiumei 李秀梅, Southwest Forestry University 西南林业大学; Professor Zhu Wang 朱望, Shantou University 汕头大学; Deputy Director/Professor Wang Zhihui 王智慧 and Dean/Professor Li Xianyi 李宪一, Yunnan University of Finance and Economics 云南财经大学.

Yunnan Minzu University 云南民族大学:

CPC Secretary Li Shiqiang 李世强, Dean/Profesor Ma Yonghong 马永红, Vice Dean Ma Yu 马瑜, Vice Dean Meng Zhiming 孟志明 (Norman Meng), Professor Sun Jing 孙静, Professor Li Xuemei 李雪梅, Sun Changliang 孙常亮 (Victor Sun), Li Qinsong 李秦松 (David Li), Li Fanghua 李方华 (David Li), Houteng Yuren 後藤裕人 (Goto Hiroto), Wu Damu 吴大睦 (Uttam Anand उत्तम आनंद), Mazlina Binti Ahmad, Yao Li 姚黎 (Jasmine Yao), Xu Xiaoming 许晓明 (Anna Xu), 张晶晶 Zhang Jing Jing (Jenny Zhang), Zhang Zhu 张蠹 (Carmen Vasquez), Xu Jianming 许建明 (Teddy Xu), Li Yongshi 李勇士 (Colin Li), Li Geyong 李革勇 (Francis Li), and the wonderfully diverse student body composed of the majority Han and multiple ethnic minorities.

Warning—Disclaimer

This book is designed to be used as an informational resource for those wishing to teach, work, and live in contemporary Chinese society. It also serves as a basic foundational guide to help educators and administrators become more acquainted with the ever changing economic giant. It is sold with the understanding that the publisher and author are not engaged in rendering legal, accounting or other professional services. If legal or other expert assistance is required, the services of a competent professional should be sought.

It is not the purpose of this manual to reprint all the information that is otherwise available to authors and/or publishers, but instead to complement, amplify and supplement other texts. You are urged to read all the available material, learn as much as possible about teaching, working and living in China, and tailor the information to your individual needs. For more information, see the many resources in the Appendix of Resources.

China literally changes every single day and this manual is not a "one size fits all" resource for every situation in the Middle Kingdom. Anyone who decides to pursue a teaching position in China must understand that every situation will be different and tailored to the individual because of credentials, experience, contracts, location, and dealing with recruiters.

Every effort has been made to make this manual as complete and as accurate as possible. However, there *may be mistakes*, both typographical and in content. Therefore, this text should be used only as a general guide and not as the ultimate source of writing and publishing information. Furthermore, this manual contains information on Chinese culture & society and the TESOL industry that is current only up to the printing date.

The purpose of this manual is to educate and entertain. The author and PinkBlot Press shall have neither liability nor responsibility to any person or entity with respect to any loss or damage caused, or alleged to have been caused, directly or indirectly, by the information contained in this book.

If you do not wish to be bound by the above, you may return this book to the publisher for a full refund.

Introduction

I absolutely love China! And I mean all of it—the good, the bad, and the ugly. China's diversity of people, regions, languages, food, culture, ritual, and etiquette can sometimes overwhelm one's senses but I think it's absolutely exhilarating! From Beijing's Wangfujing Night Market to the intense haggling with vendors at Shenzhen's Huaqiangbei to the serenity of Hangzhou's Green Lake to Xi'an's Muslim Quarter to the UNESCO designated rice terraces of Yuanyang in the Honghe region of Yunnan, the Middle Kingdom can be both fascinating and mysterious to the western traveler.

So You Wanna Teach In China? chronicles teaching English (TESOL) in Chinese society as well as Chinese culture, society, tradition, facts, resources, myth, and personal experiences---everything characteristic of the world's oldest human culture that has continuously existed over 5,000 years. Part of my motivation in writing this book is a result of fellow TESOL professional inquiries about China, student curiosity, and administrator puzzlement from both Chinese and western cultures. My goal is to enlighten the reader about TESOL in China.

Mainland China is desperate for native English-speaking TESOL professionals. With a population exceeding 1.3 billion, mainland China is quickly becoming the country with the largest English-speaking population. It is anticipated by some estimates that mainland China will have the largest English-speaking population by 2017. Even so, there continues to be an urgent need for many Chinese people to learn English so that they can participate in the global economy, travel to English-speaking nations, study abroad in English-speaking schools, establish new friendships with English speakers, and so forth. With the rise of the Chinese middle class, there is now an abundance of financial resources for extracurricular activities that many in the western nations currently enjoy.

Surprisingly, mainland China isn't the only country or region that is desperate for native English-speaking professionals. Taiwan, Russia, the Czech Republic, Saudi Arabia, South Korea, Japan, United Arab Emirates, Thailand, and Vietnam are also desperate for native English-speaking TESOL professionals.

For purposes of political correctness and cultural sensitivity, I will use "China" when referring to mainland China. If there is a reference to Hong Kong, Taiwan or Macau, I will reference these areas by their names or as "regions." *Please note that I have no personal, political, religious, or other stance regarding these regions other than referring to them as areas for potential teaching opportunities for English-speaking TESOL professionals.* I will also toggle between English teachers and

TESOL professionals depending on the reference. ESL (English as a Second Language) and EFL (English as a Foreign Language) terminology will be used as TESOL in order to include those global professionals who are certified to teach English and whose native (or first) language isn't English. The Chinese government refers to TESOL professionals as "Foreign Experts." As a China TESOL professional for more than five years, I have had the opportunity to work in government-run schools, private institutions, and the Chinese university system. For convenience, I have divided this book into four (4) major sections: Part I: Working in China; Part II: Living in China; Part III: Networking; Appendix of Resources.

In order to be successful in making a cultural and professional transition into China, these four areas are essential for the serious TESOL professional. The target audience for this book focuses on native and non-native English speakers from the major western English-speaking nations of the United States, United Kingdom, Canada, Australia, New Zealand, and South Africa. Even so, other territories, regions, and areas of the world can also benefit from reading this book. For Chinese readers, this book catalogues the processes that non-Chinese must go through in order to transition and teach in Chinese culture and society. This resource can also be helpful in preparing Chinese educators and administrators in pursuit of qualified English-speaking talent for their institutions. For western educators and administrators of colleges and universities, this resource can be used as a handbook to get a glimpse into Chinese culture, society, and to assist students in international studies programs, study abroad programs, and international student recruitment. *Chapter Fifteen* touches on Articulation Agreements and how to establish a relationship with Chinese universities.

In this first edition, I anticipate several aspects of Chinese culture and society being overlooked. I welcome any recommendations, additions, and deletions so that they may be included in the next edition. Please contact me via social media or at pinkblotpress@gmail.com. 谢谢！

Working in China

English: The International Language
China in a Nutshell
Education in China
The Chinese Visa Process
Contracts
Securing a Teaching Position
Retaining a Teaching Position
Classroom TESOL Terminology

Chapter One

English: The International Language

What You Will Learn In This Chapter:

- Basic Truths about English
- English as an International Language
- Language Acquisition Focus Areas
- Requirements for Teaching in China
- Intangible Qualifications
- Non-native, Non-white English speakers
- TESOL Teaching specialties
- Types of certifications
- Career path opportunities

Basic Truths about English

So you've been thinking about starting or changing your career to teaching English abroad in China but not exactly sure what to do or where to start? Your worries end here! This comprehensive guide is designed specifically for those who wish to Teach English to Speakers of Other Languages (TESOL) in China. By 2017, it is anticipated by some experts that China will become the largest English-speaking nation on the planet. And the English-speaking business is booming! Let's start with some basic truths about TESOL:

16 Working In China

1. English is an international language
2. English is the global business language
3. English is the communication tool for global commerce

English as an International Language

As of November 2014, China overtook the United States as the country with the largest global Gross National Product (GNP). This indicator has much impact for China as a nation because it now must be able to communicate not only with western nations but other nations globally. Since Putonghua (Mandarin) isn't the language that many nations speak, English is the way in which many Chinese will be able to compete globally in business, travel, new patents, jobs, companies, acquisitions, and so forth. According to the British Council, the United Kingdom's international organization for cultural relations and educational opportunities, the number of non-native English speakers has come to significantly outnumber the number of native speakers by a factor of three.

Language Acquisition Focus Areas

When it comes to teaching Chinese learners of English, I have identified eight (8) focus areas in which a learner has varying degrees of challenge. These focus areas include Critical

Reasoning, Grammar, Listening, Reading, Speaking, Vocabulary, Comprehension, and Writing. Depending on a learner's experience and exposure to English, the challenge area ranges from low to high with some areas variable, meaning that English learning usually varies upon the region of the country. For example, eastern China is more developed and many Chinese that reside in this area of the country tend to have a higher aptitude of English language skills or the ability and opportunity to quickly learn English. This is mainly due to the larger populations of native English speakers in the region and local governments funding special projects to improve the language learning of English to the population. A low challenge area indicates that this particular area of English (L2) acquisition is rarely a challenge in learning. A medium challenge is the middle ground for L2 language acquisition. This challenge area is the most critical area because a learner's motivation to acquire English skills will be most tested. If a learner is motivated, then he/she will improve exponentially. If the converse is true, then a learner's confidence may be waning. Therefore, teacher instruction and guidance is critical. A high challenge area indicates that a learner has major challenges in a particular area.

Age can also be a factor for Chinese learners of English.

18 Working In China

Since English has become "fashionable" and is necessary for many Chinese to actively participate in the global economy, grade school children are learning quickly and tend to be able to absorb English communication skills much quicker than adults.

	Language Acquisition Focus Areas for Chinese Learners of English		
	Focus Area	Description	Challenge Area (Low, Med, High)
1	Critical Reasoning	Critical reasoning is variable to the region which appears to correlate to the exposure to native English speakers from western countries where critical thinking is important for everyday life. The higher exposure to native English speakers, the higher probability of learning and understanding euphemisms, colloquialisms, slang, and idiomatic expressions.	Variable (depends on region)
2	Grammar	Chinese learners tend to be superb in this area. It sort of makes sense because Mandarin (L1) is similarly structured so learning the structure of English is fairly simple.	Low to Med
3	Listening	Since exposure to native English speakers can be a challenge, improving listening skills tend to be a challenge. Listening comprehension goes hand-in-hand with speaking and critical reasoning; it's crucial to understand in order to effectively respond.	Med to High

English: The International Language

	Focus Area	Description	Challenge Area (Low, Med, High)
	Language Acquisition Focus Areas for Chinese Learners of English		
4	Reading	Similar to the area of critical reasoning, listening skills are enhanced depending on the region with higher exposure to native English speakers. L1 speakers are crafty with listening to English language music, movies, TV shows, and engaging in social media. The gap between regions with fewer native English speakers versus regions with larger populations of native English speakers is closing rapidly.	Med (depends on type of reading medium)
5	Speaking	This is the most challenging area for Chinese learners because there's a large portion of the population that have zero to few opportunities to practice English with a native speaker or simply don't use English in day-to-day activities. The most critical regions of the population that require access to native English speakers are in areas less traveled: rural China.	High
6	Vocabulary	Chinese learners tend to learn vocabulary easily because English vocabulary is required on standardized tests. Major tests include the Gao Kao 高考 (gāo kǎo), College English Test (CET-4, CET-6), and Test for English Majors (TEM-4, TEM-8).	Low to Med

Language Acquisition Focus Areas for Chinese Learners of English			
	Focus Area	Description	Challenge Area (Low, Med, High)
7	Writing	Good English writing is not much of a challenge for many Chinese learners when asked to complete a task. However, essay questions (in testing) tend to be very challenging which implies that a learner's level of English comprehension and critical thinking are crucial to mastering this area.	Med
8	Comprehension	The more exposed to the English language the higher the probability of the Chinese learner improving their English capabilities. While this can be accomplished in a distance learning environment (online), in-person face-to-face instruction and immersion in an English-speaking environment are usually best for the learner.	Variable (depends on learner, region)

Once again, this is dependent on the individual and region in China as the countryside (rural China) still lags behind the larger metropolitan areas in English language acquisition. Below is a graphic that illustrates the language acquisition focus areas for Chinese learners of English. This illustration is based on my experience with hundreds if not thousands of

Chinese learners of English of all ages.

Requirements for Teaching in China

Teaching in China is a good place to start a rewarding and successful career in TESOL. Not only do you have the ability to make a positive difference in teaching English but also the opportunity to travel. China is still somewhat mysterious to foreigners and the opportunity to live and work in China allows one to kill multiple birds with one stone. Candidates with a bachelor's degree in English and/or Linguistics generally are not required to pursue a TEFL, TESOL, or CELTA certification. This is usually determined by the company or institution in which one applies.

Basic Requirements:
- Passport (with at least 6 blank pages)
- Bachelor's degree
- TEFL/TESOL/CELTA certificate (60 hrs)
- Age between 24-60 years old
- Good health*

Desired Qualifications:
- Passport (with at least 6 blank pages)
- Master's or advanced degree
- TEFL Certificate or Diploma (60-120 hrs)
- Age between 24-60 years old
- Good health*
- Teaching experience (1+ years)

As of the date of publication, a candidate must be between the ages of 24-60 years old. Many institutions have flexibility

22   Working In China

with this option depending on locale, area of the country, need, and other factors deemed necessary.

In China, "good health" indicates that one can pass a physical examination, have no communicable diseases, no STDs, and be HIV negative as of the date of this publication. Please keep in mind that regulations and guidelines in China change frequently and oftentimes without notice. For example, Ebola has more than likely been added to this list and categorized as a communicable disease. If you are applying for a teaching position from outside of China, a medical exam is required in your home country in order to be issued a Z-visa to enter China. If you are applying for a teaching position from within China, a medical exam can be administered at a local hospital or a designated medical facility specific for foreigners. Upon arrival in China, you will be required to pass another medical exam (to be paid by your employer). A successful

Intangible Qualifications:

- High adaptability to a foreign culture
- Follow Chinese laws and customs
- A "people person" able to develop and maintain good personal relationships
- Good observational skills for teaching
- Cultural openness
- High emotional intelligence
- Organizational skills
- Creativity

medical exam in China allows your employer to issue paperwork for a work permit and residence permit both which are required by law in order to teach in China.

Intangible Qualifications

Intangible qualifications are those qualifications that aren't in a job description but are necessary for everyday functions in Chinese culture and society. If one is a "people person" and able to develop, cultivate, and maintain good relationships, then there is a good chance that cultural adaptation will be relatively easy. If the converse is true, then there will be significant cultural challenges as Chinese culture and society has existed thousands of years based on good relationships. It's highly unlikely that this will change and conform to a short-term western guest. The idiomatic expression *"when in Rome, do as the Romans"* definitely applies here.

I've learned from my own experience that foreigners possessing a high emotional intelligence quotient (EQ) tend to adapt much quicker to Chinese culture and society than those with a lower EQ because of cultural openness and a zeal for wanting to adapt versus Chinese culture adapting to them. Emotional Intelligence is the ability to monitor one's own and other people's emotions, to discriminate between different emotions and label them appropriately, and to use emotional information to guide thinking and behavior. It also focuses on the individual's ability to process emotional information and use it to navigate the social environment. Chinese culture is a very social culture as well one of subtleties. The ability to observe and adapt to these subtleties is critical for cultural immersion and useful in classroom management.

Non-Native, Non-White English Speakers

For those from western countries, this seems like an odd subject to address but it's a very important subject that needs transparency and clear understanding. First of all, China does not have human resource regulations like many western countries that would find it a discriminatory practice to hire or not hire someone based on race, nationality, height, and appearance. Chinese culture has roots in mianzi 面子 (*miàn zi*) also known as *face,* which refers to one's sense of dignity or prestige in social contexts. *"To save face"* describes the lengths that an individual (or company) may go to in order to preserve their established position in Chinese society by taking action to ensure that one is not thought badly of by their peers. One of the reasons why you're asked to include a picture with your CV or resume when applying for TESOL positions is to see if you "look the part." If a company can hire a white, native English speaker, then they *appear* to be a company has the capability of hiring *"the best English candidates and we just proved it."* This process isn't personal—its business perception and this tends to be reality. While the TESOL environment in China is diverse, it's still a common perception that potential Chinese learners of English will view a company with white, native English speakers as having *a higher quality of English* versus the converse. But of course this isn't necessarily realistic in the grander scheme of TESOL and it is becoming more apparent as Chinese experience different teaching delivery styles from different types of English speakers. In reality, non-native English speakers tend to be more proficient in understanding English because of specialized training and learning English as a second language. It seems almost absurd to automatically think that because a TESOL professional is an American or British native English speaker that one can speak, understand, and deliver English lessons masterfully. This may or may not be the case.

As a non-white, native English speaker, I have been quite successful in establishing a TESOL career in China. In addition to my credentials, factors that have attributed to my success

26   Working In China

> **TESOL Tip**
>
> Guanxi 关系 (*guān xi*) refers to the benefits gained from social connections and usually extends from extended family, school friends, colleagues, and members of common groups or organizations. This concept is foundational and has a strong influence in Chinese culture and society.

include networking (known as Guanxi 关系 (*guān xì*) but more personal), high EQ, professionalism, being proactive, adaptability to Chinese culture, pursing opportunities independently in conjunction with recruiters, and setting goals. I knew that I wanted to teach in a university setting in southwestern China (Yunnan) for research and business purposes so I focused my efforts towards this goal. *Is it possible for non-white, non-native English speakers to get a teaching job in China?* Absolutely! Simply because one is a native English speaker does not guarantee that he/she can teach English. However, the reality is that you will have more of a challenge in pursuing those opportunities and salaries may be lower than your counterparts. Even so, everything in China is negotiable (salary included). My advice is to determine what your goals are and then focus on areas of the country that might help you attain those goals and aspirations. If you're ambitious, then those opportunities will present themselves. A good way to gain experience and learn the TESOL China environment is to spend a year in a large private language school. A simple Google search can assist you in this endeavor.

TESOL Teaching Specialties

There are several areas of TESOL teaching specialties in which one may pursue. It really depends on your goals—if you're simply teaching for a short period of time, just visiting and traveling China while teaching, or if you're seeking to specialize in a particular area. Regardless of your motivation, many opportunities are available. Some of the areas include:

- Academic/University
- Business/Professional
- Medical
- Children
- Finance
- Technical

Teaching children usually pays more than teaching college/university and adults; private language schools pay more than government schools but the benefits in a government school many times outweigh those of private schools.

Types of Certifications

The basic certification required to teach in China is the

28   Working In China

TEFL Certificate (Teaching English as a Foreign Language) or CELTA (Certificate in Teaching English to Speakers of Other Languages). As one of the most widely taken qualifications of its kind, the CELTA is for people with little or no previous teaching experience. This certification is provided by Cambridge English and is aligned with the Common European Framework of Reference for Languages (CEFR) which is the international standard for describing language ability. Cambridge University's testing capabilities are located at http://www.cambridgeenglish.org/.

Other certifications for career development and creating additional opportunities include the TEFL Diploma, DELTA (Diploma in English Language Teaching to Adults), TKT (Teaching Knowledge Test), and IELTS Examiner.

Career path opportunities

China is a land of opportunity and enjoying a career in TESOL has numerous opportunities. There is a need for TESOL professionals in every city in China. One distinct advantage for anyone pursuing a career in TESOL is the opportunity to travel globally and beginning or continuing your career in China is a good way to improve your credentials and teaching style.

English: The International Language   *29*

Almost every country has a need for speakers of English and depending on your individual experience, you could be quite valuable. Here are some opportunities available to those who wish to pursue a career in TESOL:

- Senior Teacher
- ESL/TESOL Center Director
- Education Director
- Academic Manager/Supervisor
- Regional Supervisor
- Academic Recruiter
- University Lecturer
- Business Consultant
- Education Consultant
- Private Tutor
- TESOL Publisher/Author
- IELTS Examiner
- Entrepreneur
- TESOL Company Start-up

Chapter Two
China in a Nutshell

What You Will Learn In This Chapter:

- Brief History of China
- Chinese Dynasties
- Modern Chinese Society
- Basic Chinese phrases for survival
- Neighboring countries
- Basic Facts About China

Brief History of China

If you want to know where the Chinese nation is going, then it is important for you to have an idea of where the Chinese nation came from and where it has been. As the world's longest continuous human civilization spanning over five-thousand years, the Middle Kingdom (as it was commonly called in the previous century) has a rich and diverse history that impresses even the naysayer. China has been through its warring periods, peaceful episodes, and not-so-proud moments. All in all, this has shaped the culture and people with effects evolving in the culmination of what is China today: a dynamic economic powerhouse that has recently overtaken the United States as the largest economy in the world.

Chinese Dynasties

While many dynasties have significance in Chinese history and culture, the dynasty with arguably the most significance is the Song Dynasty (Northern Song and Southern Song Dynasties). During this time period in Chinese history, many things evolved and those changes are most reflective of modern day Chinese culture to global outsiders. For example, the Chinese diet was different prior to the Song Dynasty. Main staples included wheat, millet and wine which had similar characteristics to western culture. However, there was a migration to rice, noodles and tea. Chinese cuisine has traditionally been the center of social interaction and continues to be in modern Chinese society. 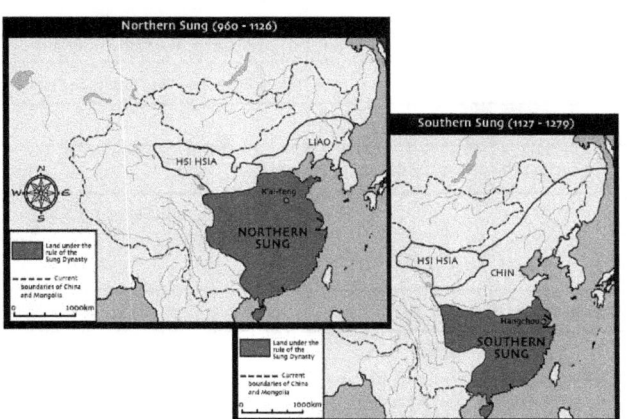 While every region has a distinct cuisine style, there are eight (8) major Chinese cuisine styles officially recognized. They include Anhui, Cantonese, Fujian, Hunan, Jiangsu, Shandong, Szechuan, and Zhejiang.

Timeline of Chinese Dynasties and Other Key Events

ca. 2100-1600 BCE	Xia (Hsia) Dynasty	
ca. 1600-1050 BCE	Shang Dynasty	Capitals: near present-day Zhengzhou and Anyang
ca. 1046-256 BCE	Zhou (Chou) Dynasty	Capitals: Hao (near present-day Xi'an) and Luoyang
	Western Zhou (ca. 1046-771 BCE)	
		Spring and Autumn Period (770-ca. 475 BCE
		Confucius (ca. 551-479 BCE)
		Warring States Period (ca. 475-221 BCE)
221-206 BCE	Qin (Ch'in) Dynasty	Capital: Chang'an, present-day Xi'an
		Qin Shihuangdi dies, 210 BCE
	Han Dynasty	
	Western/Former Han (206 BCE-9 CE)	Capital: Chang'an
		Confucianism officially established as basis for Chinese state by Han Wudi (r. 141-86 BCE)
	Eastern/Later Han (25-220 CE)	Capital: Luoyang

TESOL Tip: To remember the order of Chinese Dynasties, refer to *"The Dynasties Song"* located in the Appendix.

220-589 CE	Six Dynasties Period	Period of disunity and instability following the fall of the Han; Buddhism introduced to China
	Three Kingdoms (220-265 CE)	Cao Wei, Shu Han, Dong Wu
	Jin Dynasty (265-420 CE)	
	Period of the Northern and Southern Dynasties (386-589 CE)	
581-618 CE	Sui Dynasty	Capital: Chang'an
618-906 CE	Tang (T'ang) Dynasty	Capitals: Chang'an and Luoyang
907-960 CE	Five Dynasties Period	
960-1279	Song (Sung) Dynasty	
	Northern Song (960-1127)	Capital: Bianjing (present-day Kaifeng)
	Southern Song (1127-1279)	Capital: Lin'an (present-day Hangzhou)
1279-1368	Yuan Dynasty	The reign of the Mongol Empire; Capital: Dadu (present-day Beijing)
1368-1644	Ming Dynasty	Re-establishment of rule by Han ruling house; Capitals: Nanjing and Beijing
1644-1912	Qing (Ch'ing) Dynasty	Reign of the Manchus; Capital: Beijing
1912-1949	Republic Period	Capitals: Beijing, Wuhan, and Nanjing
1949-present	People's Republic of China	Capital: Beijing

Modern Chinese Society

Modern-day Chinese society is quite progressive in many ways. For example, meals are served family-style in restaurants and business cards are fashionable when conducting business. Chinese holidays are taken seriously as they represent China's history and culture. The most important holiday is Spring Festival, also known as Chinese Lunar New Year, where there's a mass migration of Chinese returning home 春运 (*chūn yùn*) to celebrate with relatives. Regarding social behavior, it would be considered rude if you don't drink with the host and never touch food with your hands. It's also important to avoid flashpoint topics such as Taiwan, Tibet, Xinjiang, and preference of Japanese cultural relationships over Chinese cultural relationships. Chinese gift-giving is engrained in the culture and not accepting a gift is considered very offensive. Although Chinese society is constantly changing and becoming more *western,* traditional Chinese culture is still emphasized on a day-to-day basis.

The concept of personal space is markedly different in Asian nations than it is in many western countries. Like many US citizens, the idea of *"invading my personal space"* is someone coming within an arm's length without prior consent while Chinese ideals of personal space are markedly different. It's not only normal to approach another and come within inches of them but culturally acceptable to see women holding hands or men with their arms around each other. There is also the concept of what I call *visual personal space* where individuals from western countries dislike the idea of being stared at continuously. I've learned from experience that most US citizens tend to be more uptight about being stared down

> **TESOL Tip**
> Members of the same sex holding hands or with an arm around another in public doesn't have the same meaning as it does in western culture. This cultural behavior usually designates a very close, strong friendship.

compared to Europeans. Chinese people mean no harm and many have never seen a foreigner in-person. Chinese are simply curious one should not be offended.

It is common to learn standard Mandarin in your home country and come to China and not understand a single word upon arrival. This is because there are so many dialects and regional accents in this vast nation that it's almost impossible for everyone to speak standard Putonghua (Mandarin) even though it's taught in school. My recommendation would be to ask a local for assistance whenever possible to help understand the local language and dialect.

> **TESOL Tip**
> Learn to use chopsticks because you will rarely find silverware (fork, knife, and spoon) in most restaurants unless you bring your own.

36 Working In China

Basic Chinese phrases for survival

Maslow's Hierarchy of Needs, one of the best-known theories of motivation, Abraham Maslow proposed in his 1943 paper "A Theory of Human Motivation" that human beings have needs that range from basic to complex. Beginning at the most basic needs, also known as D-needs (deficiency needs), these needs are due to a lack of something and need to be satisfied in order to avoid unpleasant feelings and to move on to higher level needs. Basic needs include breathing, food, water, sex, sleep,

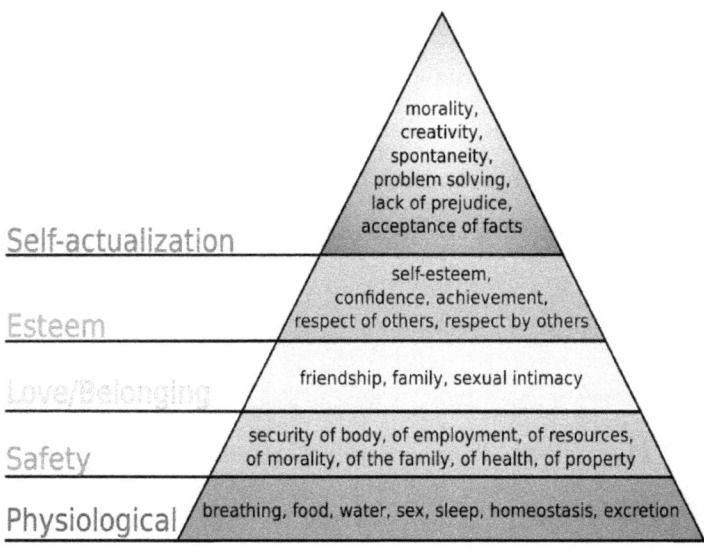

Maslow's Hierarchy of Needs.

homeostasis, and excretion. It makes sense that having these basic needs fulfilled will make Chinese cultural transition much easier. For example, understanding the difference between male 男 (*nán*) and female 女 (*nǚ*) toilets during a biological emergency is quite helpful. A few basic Chinese phrases that will be helpful during cultural transition are listed in the Appendix under *Essential Mandarin*.

> **TESOL Tip**: Public toilets generally are not well kept. Additionally, toilet tissue (also called *paper* by Chinese) is not available. Always keep paper handy for use.

Neighboring Countries

There are fourteen countries that border China. They are Afghanistan, Bhutan, India, Kazakhstan, North Korea, Kyrgyzstan, Laos, Mongolia, Myanmar (Burma), Nepal, Pakistan, Russia, Tajikistan, and Vietnam.

38   Working In China

North and Northeast countries: Mongolia, North Korea, Russia.

Silk Road countries (west of China): Afghanistan, Bhutan, India, Kazakhstan, Kyrgyzstan, Myanmar, Nepal, Pakistan, Tajikistan.

South and Southeast Asian countries: Laos, Myanmar, Vietnam.

Basic Facts About China

- The official name is the People's Republic of China 中华人民共和国 (*Zhōnghuá Rénmín Gònghéguó*).

- China is the world's oldest continuous human civilization that spans more than 5,000 years.

- China's total area is slightly smaller than the United States.

- The total population of China (1.4 billion) is more than four times that of the United States.

- The Chinese flag called *wǔ xīng hóng qí* 五星红旗 (Five Stars Red Flag) and was most recently adopted on 1 October 1949. The red background symbolized revolution and the larger star represents the Chinese Communist Party. The smaller four stars represent the workers, business people, intellectuals, and farmers.

- The Mandarin language has roughly 50,000 characters but only about 8,000 are in use; knowledge of 1,500 is necessary for basic literacy.

- China's legislature, known as the National People's Congress, has nearly 3,000 members.

40 Working In China

- Standard Putonghua, or Mandarin, is based on the Beijing dialect and is the national language.

- Chongqing is the largest city in China (and the world!) with a population ranging from 28-32 million people.

- China has had the largest and most complex economy in the world for most of the past two thousand years.

- The Chinese currency is the Renminbi (yuan) which is designated by the symbol ¥ or using CNY.

- China consists of 23 provinces, 5 autonomous regions, 4 direct-controlled municipalities, and 2 mostly self-governing special administrative regions.

- The Yangtze and Yellow Rivers are the third and sixth-longest rivers in the world simultaneously. Both rivers run from the Tibetan Plateau to the densely populated eastern seaboard.

- The Ministry of Education of the People's Republic of China oversees all educational activities, draw up strategies and policies for educational reform and development.

- China has 2,542 colleges and universities which includes 445 non-public colleges and universities.

Chapter Three
Education in China

What You Will Learn In This Chapter:

- Chinese Education Overview

- China's Ministry of Education

- State Administration of Foreign Expert Affairs (SAFEA)

- Chinese Students and Classroom Management

- Types of TESOL Teaching Assignments

Chinese Education Overview

Major differences exist in the delivery of education between Chinese and western perspectives. A major challenge for TESOL professionals seeking teaching roles in China is not only to understand and adapt to these differences but to have the capacity to instinctually integrate western teaching techniques into the Chinese framework for an enriched student-centered experience. In order to accomplish this feat, let's take a look at some of these major differences. From an early age, Chinese children are taught that education is an important foundation of Chinese culture and quickly learn to respect teachers as an authority figure. Chinese students spend the majority of their time with teachers (more than parents) and respect for the teacher is an expectation. In essence, it is understood that teachers have more authority in the guidance of a student. Chinese students study long hours, are very competitive academically, and veer towards a collective nature which in turn sometimes yields a less creative personality than their western counterparts (they must conform). Chinese students know how to study and this leads to many Chinese students being academically successful in western institutions of higher learning.

On the flipside, western children are encouraged at an early age to engage in creative, individualistic behaviors. For example, preschool children engage in coloring and games that are designed to enhance creativity. While teachers in western cultures tend to have authority in the classroom, it is not a given that students will respect the teacher because this isn't a cultural expectation. Western students do not study long hours to complete homework assignments as much as Chinese students but this doesn't preclude that western students are less competitive academically. It simply means that one system is different than the other system. One isn't necessarily better, they're just different. Another distinct advantage that western students overwhelmingly have over Chinese students is the pursuit of extracurricular activities. Student participation in athletics in grade school, high school, and college alongside academics tend to produce extraordinary individual results for the student athlete. This pursuit of excellence in itself helps students become leaders in their school, extracurricular activity, community, and eventually society.

Which is better? Which is worse? These are the wrong questions because both systems work. Although a student may progress better in one system or drastically fail in the other, both systems have their strengths and weaknesses. One thing is for certain: both systems are student-focused. This, in my opinion, is the goal of education.

China's Ministry of Education

Formally known as the Ministry of Education of the People's Republic of China, the Ministry's objective is to plan, coordinate and supervise all forms of education nationwide. This includes the development and reform of higher education on the Chinese mainland and conducting educational cooperation and exchanges with Hong Kong, Macau, and Taiwan. Additionally, the Ministry directs the work of ideology and political education, morality, physical, health, arts, and national defense education in schools nationwide while directing the construction of the Communist Party of China (CPC) in institutions of higher learning. Understanding the mission of the CPC assists TESOL professionals in university classroom management because student organizations and classrooms are structured according to CPC guidelines. For more on China's Ministry of Education, visit http://www.moe.edu.cn/.

State Administration of Foreign Expert Affairs (SAFEA)

The State Administration of Foreign Expert Affairs (SAFEA) is responsible for certifying foreign experts to work in the Chinese mainland and organizing overseas training for Chinese technical and managerial professionals. In coordination with the Public Service Bureau (PSB), SAFEA assures that all TESOL professionals are issued a work permit in addition to the necessary Z-visa for legal work entry into China. Requirements to attain a work permit vary by province. Requirements for major cities such as Beijing, Shanghai, and Shenzhen require a bachelor's degree and either two years of work experience or a TESOL certificate. To learn more, visit SAFEA at http://en.safea.gov.cn/.

Chinese Students and Classroom Management

One distinct advantage TESOL professionals can rest assured that most Chinese students possess an understanding of English reading, writing, and grammar. Most adult students have a minimum of six (6) years of English training because it is taught during primary school. The major challenge comes with spoken English because many Chinese rarely have exposure to native English speakers. Chinese language learners tend to rely on movies, television shows, talk radio, and music. As a result, English teaching in China is an opportunity for native and non-native speakers.

Types of TESOL Teaching Assignments

There are several types of TESOL teaching assignments in which one can choose according to one's goals, aspirations, and career direction. I have identified and outlined four (4) major teaching assignment areas for the TESOL professional: Government-run Schools (K-12), Public & Private Universities, Private Language Schools, and International Schools.

Government-run Schools K-12

- HIRING PERIOD: Year round
- SALARY RANGE: 6000-10,000 元
- SCHOOL HOURS: M-F, 8-5pm
- CLASS HOURS: 16-20/wk
- HOUSING: Free accommodations or stipend provided
- MEALS: Free breakfast & lunch
- All national holidays observed
- 2-hr afternoon "rest break" (12-2pm)

WORK ENVIRONMENT
- Assistant in classroom with native Chinese teacher as primary teacher
- 20-50 students per class
- Primary & secondary students (K-12)
- Follow textbook
- Must stay until 5pm (even if classes are finished for the day)

International Schools

- HIRING PERIOD: Year round
- SALARY RANGE: 12,000-30,000 元
- SCHOOL HOURS: M-F, variable
- CLASS HOURS: up to 20/wk
- HOUSING: Free accommodations or stipend provided
- MEALS: Free breakfast & lunch
- Major national holidays observed
- MAJOR FOCUS: International schools are more focused on children of expats living and working in China.

WORK ENVIRONMENT
- Primary teacher in classroom
- 20-40 students per class
- Primary & secondary students (K-12)
- Follow textbook
- Must stay until 5pm (even if classes are finished for the day)

Public & Private Universities

- HIRING PERIOD: Apr-Aug (Sept start)
- SALARY RANGE: 4500-10,000 元
- SCHOOL HOURS: M-F, variable
- CLASS HOURS: up to 20/wk
- HOUSING: Free accommodations or stipend provided
- MEALS: Semester stipend/meal card
- Major national holidays observed

WORK ENVIRONMENT
- Textbook and/or create own syllabus
- 20-40 students per class
- College-aged students (18-27yrs)
- "Lecturer" influence; enables one to use leverage for creating opportunities
- Time for research/other academic interests
- Not req'd to stay in classroom or department in off hours
- Flexible hours

Private Language Schools

- HIRING PERIOD: Year round
- SALARY RANGE: 6000-16,000 元
- SCHOOL HOURS: M-F, Sa, Su 10a-10p
- CLASS HOURS: 16-25/wk
- HOUSING: Stipend provided
- MEALS: NA (eat on your own)
- Select national holidays observed
- MAJOR PLAYERS: EF English First, Wall Street English, Disney English, Meten English, New Oriental, Shane English.

WORK ENVIRONMENT
- Follow a specific curriculum set up by the private language school
- 25-40 students per class

Chapter Four

The Chinese Visa Process

What You Will Learn In This Chapter:

- Passports

- What is a Visa?

- Types of Visas

- The New 10-Year Chinese Visa

- FAQs to the 10-Year Chinese Visa

- Reputable Chinese Visa Agents

- Visa Fee Structure

- 6-Step Process for Getting Your Chinese Visa

- Tips and Warnings

Passports

A passport is an official government document that certifies one's identity and citizenship. The passport serves two purposes:

1. To regain entry to the country of citizenship (i.e. the United States, United Kingdom, Australia, Canada, New Zealand, South Africa).

2. Is a requirement by many countries to gain entry to the country in which you are visiting.

If you are applying for a US passport for the first time, go here and follow the directions: http://1.usa.gov/1xE6uc0. The cost for a new passport for US citizens is $135 USD and is valid for 10 years. Passport information for other major English speaking nations:

    Australia: http://bit.ly/1FYIAZN
    Canada: http://bit.ly/1BtoNvw
    New Zealand: http://bit.ly/1FPBPeo
    South Africa: http://bit.ly/19XgkLs
    United Kingdom: http://bit.ly/1D4GlFr
    United States: http://1.usa.gov/1xE6uc0

What is a Visa?

Commonly known as a travel visa, a visa is a stamp or sticker placed by officials of a foreign country on a passport that allows the bearer to visit that particular country. Visas are obtained from the proper embassy or local consulate of the country to being visited. There are over 270 countries that offer travel visas and literally thousands of different types of visas available based on the country, type of visit, and length of visit.

Safety should be of great importance while traveling abroad and foreigners should be keenly aware of their surroundings at all times. For travel advisories in selected countries, refer to your country's travel advisories website for warnings. For US citizens, the US Department of State's Bureau of Consular Affairs US Visa's website provides travel warnings and updates. Visit: http://travel.state.gov for the latest updates. Travel info for major English speaking nations:

Australia: http://bit.ly/1xjJ0IN
Canada: http://bit.ly/1bAm26t
New Zealand: http://bit.ly/1Ngxx0H
South Africa: http://bit.ly/192YENx
United Kingdom: http://bit.ly/1bAmh1v
United States: http://1.usa.gov/1BPqC5Y

Types of Visas

There are several types of visas issued to foreign citizens for China. However, the most common visa for foreign teachers seeking entry into China is the Z-Visa. The Z-Visa is a single

50   Working In China

entry visa that is provided in the bearer's home country and allows the foreign teacher the opportunity to enter China legally. Upon entry, foreign teachers are required to surrender their passport to school officials (for up to 2 months) during which time the Z-Visa should be converted to a Residence Permit and Work Permit. The re-issued Residence Permit and Work Permit will be converted to a multiple-entry visa for the foreign teacher. This is a requirement in order to work in China. If a Residence and Work Permit are not filed, then you are working illegally in China. If caught, you will be deported and a "black mark" is placed on your visa record with China.

The following tables below shows the different types of Visa categories for entry into China. You will need a Visa Application Form.

Visa Category	Description of Visa
C	Issued to foreign crew members of means of international transportation, including aircraft, trains and ships, or motor vehicle drivers engaged in cross-border transport activities, or to the accompanying family members of the crew members of the above-mentioned ships.
D	Issued to those who intend to reside in China permanently.
F	Issued to those who intend to go to China for exchanges, visits, study tours and other activities.
G	Issued to those who intend to transit through China.
J1	Issued to resident foreign journalists of foreign news organizations stationed in China. The intended duration of stay in China exceeds 180 days.
J2	Issued to foreign journalists who intend to go to China for short-term news coverage. The intended duration of stay in China is no more than 180 days.
L	Issued to those who intend to go to China as a tourist.
M	Issued to those who intend to go to China for commercial and trade activities.

Visa Category	Description of Visa
Q1	Issued to those who are family members of Chinese citizens or of foreigners with Chinese permanent residence and intend to go to China for family reunion, or to those who intend to go to China for the purpose of foster care. The intended duration of stay in China exceeds 180 days. "Family members" refers to spouses, parents, sons, daughters, spouses of sons or daughters, brothers, sisters, grandparents, grandsons, granddaughters and parents-in-law.
Q2	Issued to those who intend to visit their relatives who are Chinese citizens residing in China or foreigners with permanent residence in China. The intended duration of stay in China is no more than 180 days.
R	Issued to those who are high-level talents or whose skills are urgently needed in China.
S1	Issued to those who intend to go to China to visit the foreigners working or studying in China to whom they are spouses, parents, sons or daughters under the age of 18 or parents-in-law, or to those who intend to go to China for other private affairs. The intended duration of stay in China exceeds 180 days.

Visa Category	Description of Visa
S2	Issued to those who intend to visit their family members who are foreigners working or studying in China, or to those who intend to go to China for other private matters. The intended duration of stay in China is no more than 180 days. "Family members" refers to spouses, parents, sons, daughters, spouses of sons or daughters, brothers, sisters, grandparents, grandsons, granddaughters and parents-in-law.
X1	Issued to those who intend to study in China for a period of more than 180 days.
X2	Issued to those who intend to study in China for a period of no more than 180 days.
Z	Issued to those who intend to work in China.

54   Working In China

The documentation needed to prepare before submission of your visa application to the Chinese Embassy, Consulate, or Agent includes:

→ Basic Documents

→ Supporting Documents

1. Basic Documents

(a) Passport

> An original passport with at least six months of remaining validity and blank visa pages (preferably 10), and a photocopy of the passport's data page and the photo page if it is separate.

(b) Visa Application Form (Form V.2013) and Photo

> One completed Visa Application Form with a recently-taken color passport photo (bare-head, full face) against a light background attached.

(c) Proof of legal stay or residence status (applicable to those not applying for the visa in their country of citizenship)

> If you are not applying for the visa in the country of your citizenship, you must provide the original and

The Chinese Visa Process   **55**

photocopy of your valid certificates or visa of stay, residence, employment or student status, or other valid certificates of legal staying provided by the relevant authorities of the country where you are currently staying.

(d) Photocopy of previous Chinese passports or previous Chinese visas (applicable to foreign citizens those who were Chinese citizens and have obtained foreign citizenship)

If you are applying for a Chinese visa for the first time, you should provide your previous Chinese passport held and a photocopy of its data page.

If you have obtained Chinese visas before and want to apply for a Chinese visa with a renewed foreign passport that does not contain any Chinese visa, you should present the photocopy of the previous passport's data page and the photo page if it is separate, as well as the previous Chinese visa page. (If your name on the current passport differs from that on the previous one, you must provide an official document of name change.)

Working In China

2. Supporting Documents

C Visa

A letter of guarantee issued by a foreign transport company or an invitation letter issued by a relevant entity in China.

The original and photocopy of the Confirmation Form for Foreigners Permanent Residence Status issued by the Ministry of Public Security of China.

Additional Information:

Holders of D Visa shall, within 30 days from the date of their entry, apply to the exit/entry administrations of public security organs under local people's governments at or above the county level in the proposed places of residence for foreigners' residence permits.

F Visa

An invitation letter issued by a relevant entity or individual in China. The invitation should contain:

    (1) Information on the applicant (full name, gender, date of birth, etc.)

(2) Information on the planned visit (purpose of visit, arrival and departure dates, place(s) to be visited, relations between the applicant and the inviting entity or individual, financial source for expenditures)

(3) Information on the inviting entity or individual (name, contact telephone number, address, official stamp, signature of the legal representative or the inviting individual)

G Visa

An onward air (train or ship) ticket with confirmed date and seat to the destination country or region.

J1 Visa

Visa Notification Letter issued by the Information Department of the Ministry of Foreign Affairs of China and an official letter issued by the media organization for which the journalist works.

Applicants should contact the press section of the Chinese Embassy/Consulate General in advance or and complete relevant formalities.

Working In China

Additional Information:

Holders of J1 Visa shall, within 30 days from the date of their entry, apply to the exit/entry administrations of public security organs under local people's governments at or above the county level in the proposed places of residence for foreigners' residence permits.

J2 Visa

Visa Notification Letter issued by the Information Department of the Ministry of Foreign Affairs of China or other authorized units in China and an official letter issued by the media organization for which the journalist works.

Applicants should contact the press section of the Chinese Embassy/Consulate General in advance and complete the required formalities.

L Visa

Documents showing the itinerary including air ticket booking record (round trip) and proof of a hotel reservation, etc. or an invitation letter issued by a relevant entity or individual in China. The invitation letter should contain:

(1) Information on the applicant (full name, gender, date of birth, etc.)

(2) Information on the planned visit (arrival and departure dates, place(s) to be visited, etc.)

(3) Information on the inviting entity or individual (name, contact telephone number, address, official stamp, signature of the legal representative or the inviting individual)

M Visa

(1) Documents on the commercial activity issued by a trade partner in China, or trade fair invitation or other invitation letters issued by relevant entity or individual. The invitation letter should contain:

a) Information on the applicant (full name, gender, date of birth, etc.)

b) Information on the planned visit (purpose of visit, arrival and departure dates, place(s) to be visited, relations between the applicant and the inviting entity or individual, financial source for expenditures)

c) Information on the inviting entity or individual (name, contact telephone number, address, official stamp, signature of the legal representative or the inviting individual)

Q1 Visa

For family reunion, the following documents are required:

(1) An invitation letter issued by a Chinese citizen or a foreign citizen with a Chinese permanent residence permit who lives in China. The invitation letter should contain:

> a) Information on the applicant (full name, gender, date of birth, etc.)
>
> b) Information on the visit (purpose of visit, intended arrival date, place(s) of intended residence, intended duration of residence, arrival and departure dates, relations between the applicant and the inviting entity or individual, financial source for expenditures)
>
> c) Information on the inviting individual (name, contact telephone number, address, official stamp, signature of legal representative or the inviting individual, etc.)

(2) Photocopy of Chinese ID of the inviting individual or foreign passport and permanent residence permit.

(3) Original and photocopy of certification (marriage certificate, birth certificate, certification of kinship issued by Public Security Bureau or notarized certification of kinship) showing the relationship of family members between applicant and inviting individual.

"Family members" refers to spouses, parents, sons, daughters, spouses of sons or daughters, brothers, sisters, grandparents, grandsons, granddaughters and parents-in-law.

For foster care, the following documents are required:

(1) Foster entrustment notarization issued by Chinese Embassies/Consulates General in foreign countries or Foster Care Power of Attorney notarized and authenticated in the country of residence or in China

(2) Original and photocopy of the consignor's passport (s), as well as the original and photocopy of certification (marriage certificate, birth certificate, certification of kinship issued by Public Security Bureau or notarized certification of kinship) notarized and authenticated

Working In China

certification showing the relationship between parents or guardians and children.

(3) A letter of consent on foster care issued by the trustee living in China who has agreed to provide foster care services and a photocopy of the ID of the trustee.

(4) A photocopy of the certificate indicating the permanent residence status abroad of the parent(s) when the child was born provided that either or both parents of the child are Chinese citizens.

Additional Information:

Holders of Q1 Visa shall, within 30 days from the date of their entry, apply to the exit/entry administrations of public security organs under local people's governments at or above the county level in the proposed places of residence for foreigners' residence permits.

Q2 Visa

(1) An invitation letter issued by a Chinese citizen or a foreign citizen with a Chinese permanent residence permit who lives in China. The invitation letter should contain:

    a) Information on the applicant (full name, gender, date of birth, etc.)

b) Information on the visit (purpose of visit, arrival and departure dates, place(s) to be visited, relations between the applicant and the inviting individual, financial source for expenditures)

c) Information on the inviting individual (name, contact number, address, signature etc.)

(2) Photocopy of Chinese ID or foreign passport and permanent residence permit of the inviting individual.

R Visa

The applicant should submit relevant certification in accordance with relevant regulations, and meet the relevant requirements of the competent authorities of the Chinese government on high-level talents and individuals with special skills urgently needed by China.

S1 Visa

(1) An invitation letter from the inviting individual (a foreigner who stays or resides in China for work or studies) which contains:

(2) a) Information on the applicant (full name, gender, date of birth, etc.)

b) Information on the visit (purpose of visit, arrival and departure dates, place of intended residence, relations between the applicant and the inviting individual, financial source for expenditures, etc.)

c) Information on the inviting individual (name, contact telephone number, address, signature, etc.)

(2) A photocopy of the inviting individual's passport and residence permit

(3) Original and photocopy of certification (marriage certificate, birth certificate, certification of kinship issued by Public Security Bureau or notarized certification of kinship) showing the relationship of immediate family members between applicants and inviting individual. "Immediate family members" refers to spouses, parents, sons or daughters under the age of 18, parents-in-law.

Additional Information:

Holders of S1 Visa shall, within 30 days from the date of their entry, apply to the exit/entry administrations of public security organs under local people's governments at or above the county level in the proposed places of residence for foreigners' residence permits.

S2-Visa

For visiting family members for a short period, the following documents are required:

(1) An invitation letter issued by the inviting individual (a foreigner who stays or resides in China for work or studies) which contains:

> a) Information on the applicant (full name, gender, date of birth, etc.)
>
> b) Information on the visit (purpose of visit, arrival and departure dates, place(s) to be visited, relations between the applicant and the inviting individual, financial source for expenditures, etc.)
>
> c) Information on the inviting individual (name, contact telephone number, address, signature, etc.)

(2) A photocopy of the inviting individual's (a foreigner who stays or lives in China for work or studies) passport and residence permit

(3) A photocopy of certification (marriage certificate, birth certificate or notarized certification of kinship) showing the relationship of family members between the applicant and the inviting individual. "Family members" refers to spouses, parents, sons, daughters, spouses of sons or daughters, brothers, sisters, grandparents, grandsons, granddaughters and parents-in-law.

For private affairs, documentation identifying the nature of the private affairs should be provided as required by the consular officer.

X1-Visa

(1) Original and photocopy of the Admission Letter issued by a school or other entities in China.

(2) Original and photocopy of Visa Application for Study in China (Form JW201 or Form JW202).

Additional Information:

Holders of X1 Visa shall, within 30 days from the date of their entry, apply to the exit/entry administrations of public security organs under local people's governments at or above the county level in the proposed places of residence for foreigners' residence permits.

X2-Visa

Original and photocopy of Admission Notice issued by a school or other entities in China.

Z-Visa

One of the following documents:

(1) Foreigners Employment Permit of the People's Republic of China issued by Chinese government authorities for Human Resources and Social Security, as well as Invitation Letter of Duly Authorized Entity or Confirmation Letter of Invitation issued by relevant Chinese entities.

(2) Permit for Foreign Experts Working in China issued by the State Bureau of Foreign Experts as well as Invitation Letter of Duly Authorized Entity or Confirmation Letter of Invitation issued by relevant Chinese entities.

(3) Registration Certificate of Resident Representative Offices of enterprises of foreign countries (regions) issued by Chinese authorities of industrial and commercial administration, as well as Invitation Letter of Duly Authorized Entity or Confirmation Letter of Invitation issued by relevant Chinese entities as well as Invitation

Letter of Duly Authorized Entity or Confirmation Letter of Invitation issued by relevant Chinese entities.

(4) An approval document for commercial performances issued by the Chinese government authorities for cultural affairs or Invitation Letter of Duly Authorized Entity or Confirmation Letter of Invitation issued by relevant Foreign Affairs Office of provincial governments of China.

(5) Letter of Invitation to Foreigners for Offshore Petroleum Operations in China issued by China National Offshore Oil Corporation;

Additional Information:

Holders of Z Visa shall, within 30 days from the date of their entry, apply to the exit/entry administrations of public security organs under local people's governments at or above the county level in the proposed places of residence for foreigners' residence permits.

Special Reminders

(1) The invitation letter may be in the form of fax, photocopy or computer printout, but the consular officer may require the applicant to submit the original of the invitation letter.

The Chinese Visa Process 69

(2) If necessary, the consular officer may require the applicant to provide other proof documents or supplementary materials, or require an interview with the applicant.

(3) The consular officer will decide on whether or not to issue the visa and on its validity, duration of stay and number of entries in light of specific conditions of the applicant.

(4) For further details, please visit the website of the relevant Chinese Embassy or Consulate General.

For more info on China visas, visit the Chinese Embassy or Consulate website in your home country (see *Chinese Embassies and Consulates* section).

The New 10-Year Multiple Entry Chinese Visa

As announced by US President Barack Obama in coordination with People's Republic of China President Xi Jinping 习近平 during the Asia-Pacific Economic Cooperation Leaders' Meeting (APEC) in Beijing, the 10-Year Multiple Entry Chinese visa is a new visa for frequent travelers to China and applies to all US passport holders. The purpose of the 10-Year Multiple Entry visa

70 Working In China

is to strengthen and increase economic cooperation between the United States and China while injecting billions of dollars into both economies.

FAQs to the 10-Year Chinese Visa

Below are the answers to frequently asked questions (FAQs) regarding the newly-available 10-year Chinese Visas.

1. Who is eligible for a 10-year visa?

All US passport holders can apply for a 10-year multiple-entry visa in the following categories: tourist (L), business (M), and family visit (Q2 & S2). US passport holders who apply for a student visa (X) will get 5 years. 10-year visas are not available to non-US citizens.

2. How long can I stay in China on a 10-year visa?

For 10-year multiple-entry visas, the duration of stay (the number of days you can stay in China per entry) is 60 days for L & M visas; 90 days for S2 visas and 120 days for Q2 visas.

3. Can I still get a 10-year visa if I need longer stays in China?

If you wish to stay longer than what is allowed under a 10-year visa (60 days for L & M, 90 days for S2, 120 days for Q2), you must make a special request and provide documents showing reasons for such a request. It will then be handled on a case-by-case basis by the visa officer. Please keep in mind that such requests may complicate your application.

4. Can I work in China with a 10-year visa?

No. The 10-year visa is for short term tourist or business visits only. If you want to work in China, you must obtain a work visa.

5. Does it cost more to get a 10-year visa?

No. The cost of a 10-year visa is the same as other shorter term visas for US citizens.

6. Does it take longer to get a 10-year visa?

No. The processing time remains the same. Agents usually have 4 levels of service: Regular (6+ business days), Express (4-5 business days), Rush (2-3 business days) and Emergency (24 hours).

7. Are there any special requirements for a 10-year visa?

No. The requirements for a 10-year visa are the same as that of a 1-year visa.

72 Working In China

8. My passport expires in less than 10 years. Can I still get the 10-year visa?

Yes. You can get a 10-year visa as long as your passport is valid for more than one year. Once you get a 10-year visa, you can travel on this passport even after it expires, provided it is used together with a valid new US passport bearing the same name, sex, date of birth and place of birth. If any changes are made to the above mentioned information on the new passport, you must apply for a new visa.

9. I'm going to China for a scientific conference. Can I get a 10-year visa?

No. As mentioned above, the 10-year visas are only available in the L, M, Q2 and S2 categories. Among them, the M visa is for business people going to China for business and trade purposes. People who visit China for cultural and educational exchanges and academic conferences are granted F visas, which are generally good for 6 months or 1 year.

10. The Chinese Visa Application Form does not have a 10-year option. What do I do?

You can make a request for a 10-year visa on the Chinese Visa Application Form. On Section 2.2, you can choose "Other" and write "10 Years" in the blank space.

11. I just received a Chinese visa that is good for 1 year. Can I have it changed to 10 years?

No. The Chinese Embassy will not issue a new visa if your current visa has more than 3 months of validity remaining. You should use your current visa and apply for a new one when the current visa expires, at which time you will be able to get a 10-year visa as long as you apply for an L, M, Q2 or S2 visa.

Reputable Chinese Visa Agents

Using an agent to process your Chinese Visa can be beneficial depending on your circumstances. For example, if you're in a rush an agent offers expedited service for your needs. If you're not in a hurry, you can request regular visa processing service which usually takes between 7-8 business days. The advantage of using an agent is that the agent is usually up-to-date on the latest processes, procedures, and updates necessary for visa processing. Additionally, China has specific requirements when it comes to processing visas. For example, if the visa application is sent to the wrong jurisdictional office, it can be rejected or denied which can cause a delay in your travel plans. If you are familiar with Chinese visa processing and Embassy or Consulate procedures, you can simply enter the Chinese Embassy or Consulate in your jurisdiction and process the visa application yourself. Please note that China visa applications should be typed before submission. While I do not endorse a specific agent to process a Chinese Visa, I have used a couple of agents in the United States that have worked well for me. They are:

1. China Visa Service Center (http://www.mychinavisa.com/)
2. A Briggs Passport & Visa Expeditors (http://www.abriggs.com/)

Visa Fee Structure

Fees for obtaining a Chinese Visa vary from country to country. The fee structure is based on reciprocal agreements with China and the foreign nation. At the date of publication, US citizens pay the highest dollar amount for a Chinese Visa. The table below illustrates the general fee structure for Chinese Visas:

Number of Entries	U.K. Citizens	U.S. Citizens	Citizens of other countries
Single entry	£30	£90 ($140 USD)	£20 ($30 USD)
Double entries	£45	£90 ($140 USD)	£30 ($45 USD)
Multiple entries for 6	£90	£90 ($140 USD)	£40 ($60 USD)
Multiple entries for 12 months or more than one year	£180	£90 ($140 USD)	£60 ($90 USD)

The Chinese Visa Process   **75**

Note: Fees are paid by money order, cashier's check, or Credit Card (Visa or MasterCard only). Cash or personal/company check is not accepted at most Embassies and Consulates.

6-Step Process for Obtaining Your Chinese Visa

Six (6) steps to get your Chinese Visa:

- Have passport, will travel. Be sure to have at least 6 months remaining on your passport and 10 blank pages. If you do not have a passport, apply for a new one before continuing through this process. If you do not have at least 10 blank pages before applying, contact a Chinese Embassy official to see if you need to add pages to your passport before continuing through the process.

- Say "Cheese." Submit 2 recently taken color passport photographs (bare-headed, full-faced, eyes showing) against a light background. Passport dimensions are 2"x2" (48mm x 33mm). Many drugstores have this passport photo service (i.e. Walgreens, Walmart, CVS, Rite-Aid, Boots, London Drugs).

- Complete the [Visa Application Form (Form V.2013)](#) of the People's Republic of China.

76   Working In China

- Include all materials with the application for processing (Passport, Invitation Letter, Work Permit, Contract, other documentation).

- Go to the Chinese Embassy/Consulate in your jurisdiction or submit materials to an Agent (passport included).

- Pay Visa Application Fee (according to your country fee schedule).

Chapter Five

Contracts

What You Will Learn In This Chapter:

- Contract Fundamentals

- Contract Anatomy

- Contract Scams

- Contract Tips

Contract Fundamentals

The length of a typical TESOL contract is one year. However, this is variable depending on the company or institution. Since visas and residence permits are approved and issued by the State Administration of Foreign Expert Affairs (SAFEA) for one year, it makes sense that companies and institutions issue one year contracts. A few months prior to the end of the contractual period, a TESOL professional is usually approached by the employer with an option to renew for an additional year. Standard items in a contract for TESOL professionals include salary information, length of the contract, visa sponsorship guidelines and explanation, outlined medical responsibility, housing information, job duties, work hours,

78   Working In China

arbitration, rules & regulations regarding Chinese law, and personal conduct for TESOL professionals. Contractual expectations include housing, payment of return airfare at the end of the contract, arrival airfare reimbursement—you pay out-of-pocket to come to China and get reimbursed that amount within a certain period of time (usually after you are issued a working visa and residence permit which takes roughly 60 days if the process is started immediately upon your arrival to China). Keep in mind that if you do not complete the contractual period of one year, the employer is not obligated to purchase an airline ticket for return to your home country. You should not have to foot any expense for airfare either coming or leaving China. If you are asked to pay airfare without reimbursement, then you should reexamine the company or university. This process is a rule-of-thumb for TESOL professionals in China as of the date of publication of this book. While policies change frequently, I do not anticipate this particular policy changing anytime soon because China continues to be desperate for TESOL professionals and educating it's countrymen to compete globally.

What is also rule-of-thumb is for employers to provide housing accommodations for TESOL professionals. A standard apartment/flat includes at least one bedroom, living room, kitchen, bathroom (western-style), and balcony/porch for laundry. Instead of an employer providing housing, a stipend may be provided. This amount (in Chinese RMB) will be outlined in the contract. It is important to note that many apartments in China require you to pay first month's rent, last month's rent, security deposit, and an agent's fee (usually one-half of one month's rent) before being given the keys to the apartment. *Chapter Eleven* outlines this process in more detail. Additions and subtractions of this standard housing procedure will depend on the city/town, teaching assignment, and employer. *Be sure to have this item outlined in your contract.* Unlike many western countries, there is very little legal recourse for foreign guests so it's important to have everything outlined in the contract. *Remember that everything in China is negotiable and if you don't ask for something, it will never be considered.*

TESOL Tip	Everything in China is negotiable. This is a cultural difference between China and western nations where negotiating set pricing can be "uncomfortable" even in interview situations.

80   Working In China

Contract Anatomy

It is standard practice in China that all contractual agreements for TESOL professionals be displayed in both English and Mandarin. If a contract is lacking either language, it is recommended that you request a contractual agreement that displays both English and Mandarin before review.

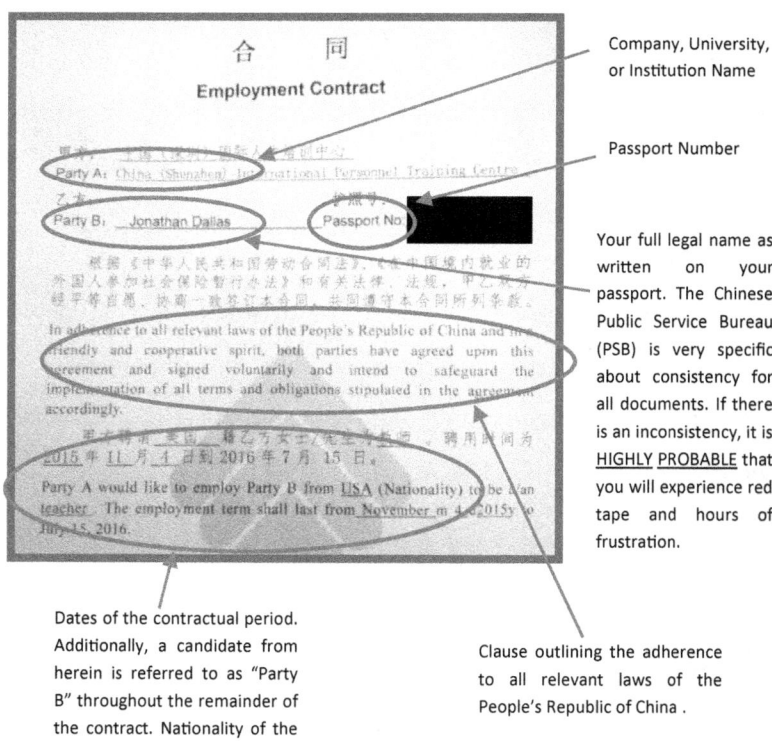

Company, University, or Institution Name

Passport Number

Your full legal name as written on your passport. The Chinese Public Service Bureau (PSB) is very specific about consistency for all documents. If there is an inconsistency, it is HIGHLY PROBABLE that you will experience red tape and hours of frustration.

Dates of the contractual period. Additionally, a candidate from herein is referred to as "Party B" throughout the remainder of the contract. Nationality of the candidate is also displayed.

Clause outlining the adherence to all relevant laws of the People's Republic of China .

Contracts 81

Pay close attention to the **Termination clause.** This is for both the protection of Party A as well as Party B. It is standard practice that if there is a termination of the contract by either Party that the Party terminating the agreement will have to pay "damages" for the termination. Dollar amounts vary according to the Company, University, or Institution.

> liquidated damages to Party A according to the next item. Party B should cooperate with Party A with the cancellation of the Foreign Expert Certificate and Residence Permit. If Party B resigns or is dismissed, he/she should finish the resignation procedure before claiming his/her last pay check.
>
> (3) 当事人一方不履行合同或者履行合同义务不符合合约定条件，即违反合同时，应当向另一方支付 1000 美元（或相当数额的人民币）的违约金。因乙方原因造成第三方损失的，应由乙方全额赔偿，甲方无责任。乙方不予赔偿时，甲方有权扣发乙方工资以抵支第三方损失。
>
> If either Party A or Party B fails to execute or underperform the duties stipulated in this agreement, that is to say, breached the agreement, it will be required pay off **liquidated damages of up to $1000USD** for relevantly exchanged amount of RMB to the other party. Party A takes no financial responsibility for Party B's actions. Any action by Party B that results in damage to property or other financial loss shall be repaid fully by Party B. If Party B does not cover these costs in a timely manner, Party A reserves the right to deduct these costs from Party B's salary.

In this case, liquidated damages (termination fee) ranges up to $1000 USD.

TESOL Tip

If one leaves China on bad terms, your name is placed on a "Blacklist" with the Public Service Bureau (PSB). This may either prevent you from re-entering the country or legally working with another employer.

82   Working In China

The Chinese RED STAMP makes this document official. Every Contractual Agreement should have a RED STAMP accompanying it in order to be official.

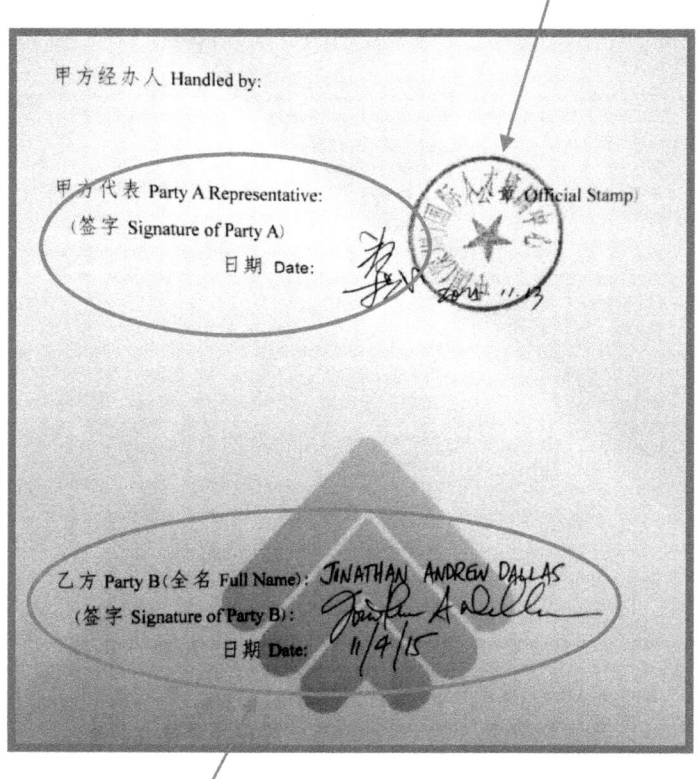

Signing of the Contractual Agreement. You (Party B) are required to print, sign, date, and in many cases include your passport number in the signatory. The Visa Process cannot begin unless there is a signed contract.

Party A (Company, University, or Institution representative) is also required to sign this form in order for the Visa Process to begin.

Contracts

中国(深圳)国际人才培训中心

邀请函

中华人民共和国驻美国大使馆（总领馆/领事馆/处）：
The embassy (consulate general/consulate/office) of the P.R.China in the U.S.A.;

本单位中国(深圳)国际人才培训中心邀请 JONATHAN ANDREW DALLAS (姓名)将于 2016 年 2 月 17 日（入境时间）来华，停留 000 天，从事任职就业活动，需申请 3 个月有效 1 次入境签证。

China (Shenzhen) international personnel training center has invited JONATHAN ANDREW DALLAS altogether 1 person to come to China on 2016.2.17 and stay for 000 days to work, and need to apply single entry (or entries) visa valid for 3 months.

邀请单位联系人：韩姜娜 联系电话：▇▇▇
Contact person of the company: ▇▇▇
Tel: ▇▇▇

请使馆配合办理相关工作证件。
Please afford cooperation and assistance to transact relative work certificates.

单位负责人签字：
日期：2016.1.20

A formal letter from the company/organization to the Embassy or Consulate General /Consulate/Office of the People's Republic of China in your home country is necessary for visa processing.

84   Working In China

A Work Permit is required to present along with an Invitation Letter to the Chinese Embassy/Consulate in your home country. Your Chinese Visa cannot be processed without these documents.

Contracts

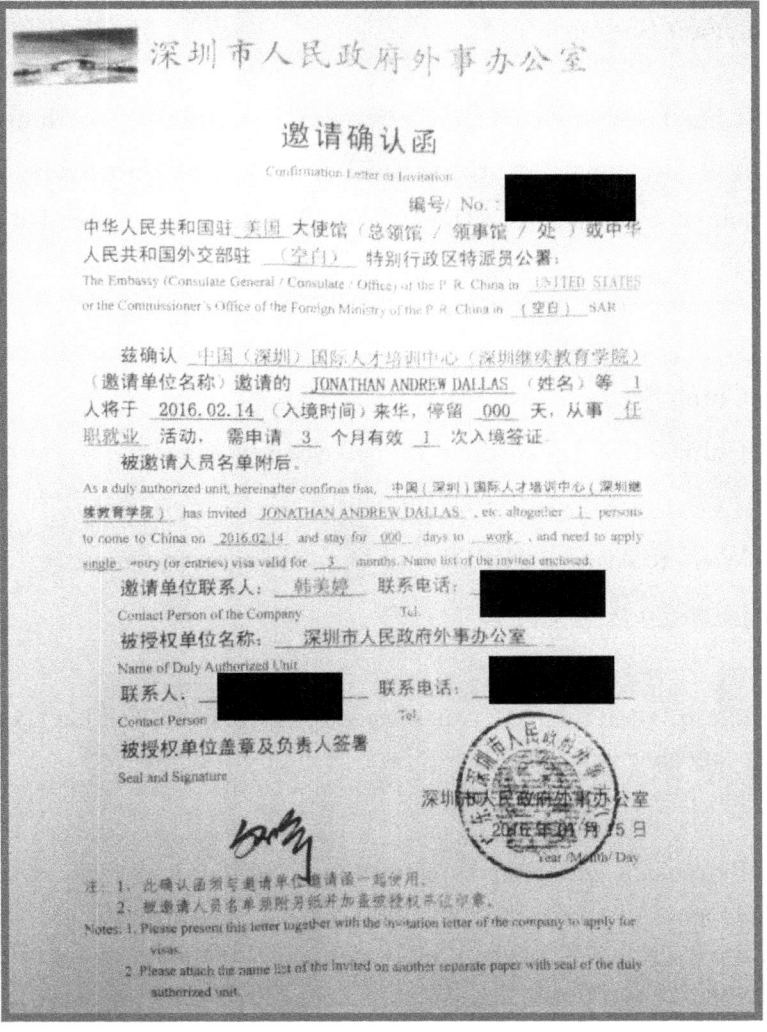

An Invitation Letter must be sent to the address in your home country from your prospective employer prior to sending to the Chinese Embassy/Consulate in your home country for Visa Processing.

Contract Scams

It has been reported that 1 in every 5 recruiters are identity thieves. Be smart, aware, and ask questions. Below are a few websites compiled by the China Foreign Teachers Union (CFTU) regarding on-going and potential TESOL scams.

- China Scam Watch: http://bit.ly/1EIttzR
- China TESOL Recruiter Cloned Scam Websites: http://bit.ly/1xEfPk0
- Ways to Avoid a TESOL employment scam in China: http://bit.ly/1F0basl

Things to remember if you suspect that a recruiter isn't who they say they are:

1. Request a recruiter to complete a verification form if you suspect that they are not legitimate. Visit www.facebook.com/pinkblotpress to download a recruiter verification form.
- **NEVER** send money if asked.

Contract Tips

> **TESOL Tip**

- TESOL Professionals are officially called Foreign Experts by the Chinese Public Service Bureau 公安局 (*Gōng'ānjú*).

- Read everything. This sounds boring (and it usually is!) but it will be well worth your time and effort in the long run if you read everything.

- Everything is negotiable. **EVERYTHING.** If you don't ask, then you won't receive and this is especially true in China.

- Never sign a contract without both English and Mandarin languages. Request a contract with both languages so that you can have some type of recourse.

- Typical items in a contract include salary information, length of contract, visa sponsorship explanation, medical responsibility, housing information, job duties, work hours, arbitration, rules & regulations regarding Chinese law, and your personal conduct as a Foreign Expert (TESOL professional).

- Western and western-looking Recruiters are just as likely to scam you as Chinese Recruiters. Don't be fooled.

Chapter Six

Securing a Teaching Position

What You Will Learn In This Chapter:

- Inquiring about Teaching Positions

- Setting Proper Expectations

- TESOL job websites

- The TESOL Blacklist

- Tips and Warnings

Inquiring about Teaching Positions

There are many ways to find TESOL positions in China because of the high demand for English teachers. Depending on the area of the country, the demand will vary. Below are some ways in which to inquire about teaching roles:

- *Find the person-in-charge or the person hiring.* Many times it's the same person.

- *For government or private schools, contact recruiters.* For universities, contact the Dean of the School of Foreign Languages or the Deputy Director of the School of International Affairs.

- *Send a basic cover letter request to teach via email or telephone.* Telephone is the most reliable method of reaching someone in China.

- *Set up a QQ account.* Go to http://www.imqq.com (international English version) and create an account. Many recruiters can be in contact with you through writing, video, or voice anywhere on the planet. For ease, you can also send files instantly to a trusted, verified employer (e.g. scanned passport first page, photographs, CV).

- *Set up a WeChat mobile account.* Many employers are mobile now are always on-the-run. In order to stay in contact, you can set up a WeChat account where you may also receive instant mobile updates. Go to http://www.wechat.com for account setup. My WeChat account is *"DallasRox"* and you are welcome to connect with me.

Setting Proper Expectations

As a teenager, I was fortunate enough to participate in Junior Achievement, an organization that teaches high school students about business. One of the most important skills I learned while in Junior Achievement was communication—

getting your product out to the consumer. In order to assist with this process, I was fortunate enough to be selected to participate in the Dale Carnegie course which is a public speaking course. While I learned several concepts throughout the 16-week course, the concept that had the most impact on me was the *Three C's: Never Criticize, Condemn, or Complain.* This advice has been helpful throughout my personal and professional life and China is no exception. What I didn't realize prior to arriving in China more than 5 years ago was that the Three C's is a foundational component of Chinese culture even though my Dale Carnegie instructors probably never had any idea.

One thing to remember as you embark upon your TESOL career in China is that you are here as a Foreign Expert—to teach English to smart, attentive students that depend on you. Chinese people take education and this important responsibility serious and you should, too. This means preparing your teaching style, classroom management, and coaching skills accordingly. Remember that you are the *expert* and your students and colleagues will be looking to you for advice regarding TESOL. Other expectations you should consider while in the classroom:

- *Avoid political or religious discussions.* You are a teacher, not the President of the United States or a Christian televangelist.

- *Remember that TESOL is the main reason why you're in China, not travel.* Work first, then play.

- *Develop strong working relationships.* China is a relationship-oriented country and connections are very important in day-to-day life. It would be wise to develop these connections as soon as possible for easier cultural adaptation.

- *Never discuss Taiwan or Tibet.* These two regions are an internal Chinese matter and should not be discussed as a foreign guest. I'd advise adding "disputed islands in the South Pacific" and Xinjiang to this list.

- *Observe and practice the Three C's:* Never Criticize, Condemn, or Complain. No one likes anyone who complains *especially* the Chinese. You will be avoided like the plague.

- *Adhere to China's laws and regulations.* If you're not sure about what is right or wrong, consult your Foreign Affairs Officer.

- *Conduct yourself and your country with respect.* You are an ambassador for your country. Remember that Chinese and others are watching you and will form an opinion of you and your country according to your actions.

- *Take responsibility for your actions*—both good and not so good.

TESOL job websites

There are several TESOL websites in China but one must always be aware of potential teacher scams. Some of the TESOL websites that I've used include:

Angela's ESL Café: http://anesl.com/schools/index.asp

British Council (UK): http://www.britishcouncil.org/

Dave's ESL Café: http://eslcafe.com/

Gold Star TEFL: http://goldstarteachers.com/

NAFSA: Association of International Educators: http://www.nafsa.org

Oxford Seminars:

http://www.oxfordseminars.com/esl-schools-directory/asia/china

Serious Teachers: http://seriousteachers.com/

TESL (Canada): http://www.tesl.ca/

TESOL International (US): http://www.tesol.org/

The TESOL Blacklist

Foreign guests have few options or recourse when it comes to work or contract disputes in China. Even with good relationships, it is sometimes a challenge to deal with companies, institutions, or recruiters that may not "follow the rules." As a result, a TESOL Blacklist has been created by the China Foreign Teachers Union (CFTU) in Beijing. Visit this link to see if a company, institution, or recruiter is on this list. http://bit.ly/1xjZII6.

According to the CFTU, a company, institution, or recruiter is placed on the TESOL Blacklist because:

◊ three (3) or more people would have had filed a complaint within a year
◊ complaints did not get resolved by the company, institution, or recruiter

94 Working In China

There are thousands of companies, institutions, and recruiters in China and this list predominately applies to those entities in Beijing. In order to be sure that you're not getting into a situation that is not a WIN-WIN, I would recommend asking many questions and request verification if you suspect that something doesn't feel right. A company, institution, or recruiter will not have a problem answering your questions if they are legitimate. For agencies and employers who are unable to legally secure proper permits to bring employees to China to work legally will many times issues *travel visas* or other types of visas. If you are coming to China to teach, your employer should be able to help you secure a Z-visa. If not, be weary of this situation because you just may be coming to China illegally. Any work in China without a work-type residence permit is illegal.

Tips and Warnings

TESOL Tip
- **NEVER** pursue a teaching position if the "employer" asks you to pay money in any form. This is an illegal practice in China and you will more than likely lose your "investment." You will never have to pay a "deposit" or "down payment" in order to teach in China.

- Request a verification letter from an Agent/Recruiter if you suspect a scam. A form can be retrieved from the publisher's website at www.facebook.com/pinkblotpress.

- If you suspect that a recruiter isn't legitimate, **NEVER** send your personal information until you have verified who they are with a proper (1) Ministry of Education Registration number, (2) SAIC License Number, and (3) Scan of the front and back of their Chinese identification Card with their Chinese name. Chinese identification cards do not have English or pinyin typed on the front or back. *All characters are in Mandarin.*

- Western and western-looking Recruiters are just as likely to scam you as Chinese Recruiters. Don't be fooled.

- Conducting a proactive job search with multiple recruiters and resources is your best option at selecting a great teaching position.

- If seeking a college/university position, begin your search in December or January of the year prior to the Fall semester in which you're seeking employment. You will receive the best opportunities when you begin this early.

Chapter Seven
Retaining a Teaching Position

What You Will Learn In This Chapter:

- Classroom Management

- Extracurricular Activities

- Evaluations

- Letters of Reference

- Valuable Tips

Now that you understand how to secure a TESOL position and set proper expectations, let's discuss how to keep that great position. To start off, first impressions are lasting ones especially in Chinese culture.

Classroom Management

Classroom management is the process of ensuring that classroom lessons run smoothly despite behavior to the contrary. Some of the best students that I've taught have been from Asia because education is taken very serious in the culture. Unlike western students, Chinese students spend more time studying in school and in other academic venues than living at home with their parents. Chinese students also *know how to study* and they do it extremely well. The western concept of classroom management tends to refer to dealing with disruptive students. *This rarely happens in China.* I have listed a few suggestions for TESOL professionals when engaging students in the classroom:

- *Engage your students and keep things fresh.* We all have had teachers that are so boring that we wished that we were anywhere besides *that* classroom. How about being so excited to attend a cool, fun class that we wouldn't miss it for the world? Teaching Chinese learners is no different except you may have to engage learners more directly because it's sometimes difficult to read their facial expressions (or lack thereof) if "they get it." Many times, Chinese learners will provide a default response of *"yes, I understand"* even though they do not because they're taught to conform in the Chinese educational system and do not want to appear "stupid" or lose face (面子 *miàn zi*) to the foreign teacher.

- *Show learners what you expect from them.* This can occur through writing on the blackboard, PPT, speaking, listening, social media, and so forth.

- *Evaluate constantly in multiple venues.* Generally speaking, I've learned that male Chinese students tend to be slightly behind their female counterparts when it comes to spoken English in the classroom environment. Male students tend to not want to speak in class so I provide other venues to listen to them and engage them. For example, you can play basketball or table tennis and *"secretly"* evaluate how they respond to you and their teammates. Another venue could be listening and speaking to learners in an English Corner away from the classroom. <u>FACT</u>: *Different environments produce different results.*

- *Acknowledge when you get what you want.* Acknowledge the learner with a simple "good" or "很好 (hen hao) very good" when the learner accomplishes a task. This goes a long way in developing the confidence of the Chinese language learner and it makes you look like a star teacher!

- *Be prepared with a lesson plan.* Chinese learners are very astute and have an expectation that teachers will be responsible for their learning. If you come to class unprepared, this reflects poorly on you and could act as a demerit against your TESOL assignment. Remember: *If you stay ready, you don't have to get ready.*

- *Acknowledge inappropriate behavior.* While this rarely occurs in the Chinese learning environment (cultural), this behavior can be managed by adhering to the lesson plan. Physically moving close to the offending student during classroom exercises or directly asking a question pertaining to the lesson usually corrects the inappropriate behavior.

Extracurricular Activities

Participation in extracurricular activities can be fun, exciting, and vastly compliment your classroom teaching. Though not required, participating can also improve the student-teacher relationship while solidifying your teaching contractual obligations for the next term. Chinese administrators absolutely enjoy foreign teacher participation to engage students and provide additional opportunities to learn and practice their spoken English.

More and more frequently, English learners in China today are no longer waiting for their foreign teachers to offer additional speaking opportunities. Instead, they're soliciting public places that TESOL professional frequent such as coffee shops, shopping malls, western restaurants, and sporting activities. Academic competition is fierce and the first to engage a foreigner, the better the opportunity is to improve their spoken English by establishing a *friendship*. Here's several ideas to help provide additional English speaking opportunities for Chinese learners:

- *English Corner*. This is a popular activity for learners to use the English learned in class in an open, non-judgmental environment.

- *FLTRP Cup English Public Speaking Contest*. This activity is a provincial and national competition that encourages students to write an original speech and deliver it in a competitive venue. Participation in this event helps to improve confidence in speaking and overcoming objections during the question phase.

- *Sports Competition*. Part of the Chinese lifestyle is to include exercise every morning. Asking students to come exercise in a sporting activity is quite normal.

- *Dinner Activity*. Food has a significant role in Chinese culture and a pair of chopsticks can go a long way. You can learn about each other through cultural exchange.

Evaluations

Someone is always watching your behavior and teaching style in China so it's best to always be on your best behavior. The evaluation period extends beyond the learning environment. Many times there are no formal evaluations. Private language schools tend to conduct formal evaluations because they are directly attached to promotions and salary raises. Learning environments like the university or public schools have both formal and informal evaluations for TESOL professionals. If a third party company is involved, there is usually an evaluative process involved. It's best to consult about the evaluation process prior to accepting a TESOL role. I discuss this in more detail in *Chapter Fifteen, Building a Professional Network*.

Letters of Reference

The role of the TESOL professional is global and your next assignment can be anywhere on the planet. Since many companies and recruiters do not communicate with a standard platform, letters of reference (LOR) are quite useful. What LORs do is market you to potential employers by providing an account of your work style and habits in your previous role.

102 Working In China

This is becoming a requirement for TESOL professionals as competition increases. For Chinese employers, many require a LOR while others simply want to interview in-person. Serious institutions require a LOR because they want to learn how you performed in your previous role.

Valuable TESOL Tips

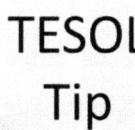

- In the Chinese learning environment, teachers are constantly evaluated by the students. This carries the most weight in determining if the teacher is a good fit for the students and institution.
- Singling out Chinese students in the learning environment is generally not appropriate because learners are not accustomed to individualism like their western counterparts. Assign work in groups and mix groups with advanced, intermediate, and below average language learners. This way, the group works together to help each other improve over time.

- Write your own Letter of Reference (LOR) template and give it to your employer prior to the end of your TESOL assignment. He/she can edit your LOR template to fit your position and abilities. This presents you as being proactive and saves your employer a lot of time in writing and processing a LOR in English.

- Conducting a proactive job search with multiple recruiters and resources is your best option to accepting a great teaching position.

- If seeking a university position, begin your search in December or January of the year prior to the Fall semester in which you're seeking employment. You will receive the best opportunities when you begin this early.

- Teacher salaries are higher in cities like Beijing, Shanghai, Guangzhou, and Shenzhen. However, the cost of living is also quite high in these cities.

Chapter Eight

Classroom TESOL Terminology

What You Will Learn In This Chapter:

- Classroom Language

- Teaching Acronyms

- Acronyms In The TESOL Environment

Classroom Language

The main reason why TESOL professionals are hired to teach in China is to expose Chinese learners to spoken English. As previously mentioned, many Chinese have very few opportunities to interact with foreign English speakers and the TESOL professional assists in the process of helping learners improve their English communication skills. Depending on the learner's English language level, it may be necessary to *help the student along* by speaking what I call *Guided Mandarin*. Guided Mandarin *is select vocabulary, idiomatic expressions, and culture-related terminology and expressions used to help guide the Chinese language learner to understand the context in which the English language is used.* It can also be used to assist the learner in recognizing similar expressions and cultural connotations in Chinese culture. For example, the idiomatic expression *"when in Rome, do as the Romans"* is almost identical to the idiomatic expression "入乡随俗 (*ru xiang sui su*)" used in Chinese culture. The literal meaning of 入乡随俗 is *"to adhere to the local custom when you are there."* Similarly, the idiomatic expression *"to kill two birds with one stone"* is expressed in Mandarin as "一石二鸟 (*yi shi er niao*)" which literally means *"one stone, two birds."* Both of these idiomatic expressions are so similar that the TESOL professional can use these similarities as an opportunity to encourage student learning while understanding the cultural positioning of these expressions. The more you learn about the student's culture, the more you understand the student and develop a positive connection conducive to the learning environment.

Teaching Acronyms

Depending on the TESOL assignment, teaching acronyms can be tossed around frequently without explanation. In my experience, I've learned that many of these teaching acronyms tend to be used frequently in private language schools in the office and professional development environments. Even so, this is industry terminology that needs to be understood for the TESOL professional's own professional development. Major acronyms used include:

> **CALL** - Computer Assisted Language Learning
>
> **DOS** - Director of Studies at a language school or academy
>
> **EAP** - English for Academic Purposes
>
> **EMT** - English Mother Tongue
>
> **ELL** - English Language Learner
>
> **ESP** - English for Specific Purposes
>
> **L1** - a student's first/native language
>
> **L2** - the language that a student is currently learning
>
> **LEP** - Limited English Proficient

Acronyms In The TESOL Environment

Common acronyms that are used in the TESOL environment are used in publications, newsletters, and organizations.

CELTA: Certificate in English Language Teaching to Adults, administered by the University of Cambridge Local Examinations Syndicate and Royal Society of Arts, based in England. This is a specific, brand name TEFL certificate course.

EAP: English for academic purposes.

EFL: English as a foreign language -- English language programs in non-English-speaking countries where English is not used as the lingua franca. It is also used in some U.S. university programs where international students study English and are likely to return to their home countries after graduation or finishing course work.

ELL: English language learner -- often used to refer to a student in an ESL or EFL program.

ELT: English language teaching or training -- used internationally.

ESL: English as a second language -- English language programs in English-speaking countries where students learn English as a second language.

ESP: English for specific purposes.

ESOL: English to speakers of other languages -- used to describe U.S. elementary and secondary English language programs. It is also used to designate ESL classes within adult basic education programs and as a general term for ESL/EFL.

IEP: Intensive English program.

LEP: Limited English proficient -- often used to describe the language skills of students in ESL or EFL programs.

RSA: Royal Society of Arts, part of the Oxford Cambridge RSA group which administers a variety of exams for lifelong learning. Visit http://www.ocr.org.uk/ for more information.

TEFL: Teaching English as a foreign language -- often used to refer to teacher education programs in EFL.

TESL: Teaching English as a second language -- often used to refer to teacher education programs in ESL.

TESOL: Teaching English to speakers of other languages -- a professional activity that requires specialized training. It is also the name of the association, Teachers of English to Speakers of Other Languages.

TOEFL: Test of English as a Foreign Language -- an exam administered worldwide to international students applying to U.S. institutions of higher education.

UCLES: The University of Cambridge Local Examinations Syndicate (UCLES), an institution of the University of Cambridge, Cambridge, United Kingdom. UCLES offers five main EFL examinations covering a range of abilities for EFL *students*.

Living in China

China's Big 3
Mainland Banking and Finance
Housing
Grocery Stores and Restaurants
APPs for Survival
For Education Directors & Administrators
Building a Professional Network

Chapter Nine
Technology and Telecom China's Big 3

What You Will Learn In This Chapter:

- The Big 3 Overview

- SIM Cards

- The Great Internet Wall of China

- Virtual Private Networks

The Big 3 Overview

We all know of the automotive industry's *Big 3* in Detroit and its importance to the American manufacturing industry. China also has a *Big 3* that is critical to the telecommunications industry countrywide. In 2008, the telecommunications industry was reorganized to allow three (3) companies to offer mobile and wireless service: China Mobile (中国移动 *zhong guo yi dong*), China Unicom (中国联通 *zhong guo lian tong*), and China Telecom (中国电信 *zhong guo dian xin*). These are the only mobile telecom solutions available for consumers.

112 Living In China

SIM Cards

China mobile service providers use a modified version of Global System for Mobiles (GSM) and Code Division Multiple Access (CDMA) technology. These are the two basic technologies in telecom. CDMA carriers use a network-based white list to verify subscribers while GSM carriers use Subscriber Identity Module (SIM) cards. CDMA technology is predominately used in the United States while the rest of the planet uses GSM technology. This can pose a problem for US citizens relocating to China if they use a CDMA-based phone. US-based CDMA carriers are Sprint and Verizon while AT&T and T-Mobile are GSM carriers. Even though Sprint and Verizon phones have SIM cards, they are usually there to support Verizon's 4G LTE networks and may not  work in China's mobile networks by simply swapping the SIM card.

The most popular company, China Mobile, operates on a modified CDMA network. Many of the services provided on this network can operate similar to a GSM network where the SIM card can be removed from the current device and placed into another device with your phone number and information intact. 4G is also available. Of the three networks, China Mobile ranks first, China Unicom second, and China Telecom is the least preferred mobile network.

The Great Internet Wall of China

Historically, the Great Wall of China was built over several hundred years to protect the country from invaders from the north. *The Great Internet Wall of China* (also known as the *Great Firewall*) is a euphemism describing the Chinese government's censorship of information deemed objectionable. The area of government that is tasked to censor objectionable information is the Ministry of Industry and Information Technology (MIIT). Filtering software detecting sensitive words in data moving through the network breaks the connection by sending a reset command so that the user can't access the sensitive information.

The Ministry of Industry and Information Technology has

114   Living In China

created a list of sensitive topics and keywords which changes frequently. It is nearly impossible to anticipate what words are on this list but foreign expats who are veterans of China can usually guess what words can potentially end up on this list. Another way to guess which words are probably on this list is to simply do a search without the use of a Virtual Private Network (VPN). Western social media that currently cannot be accessed on the Chinese mainland without the use of a VPN include Facebook, Twitter, Google, Google Plus, Gmail, Flickr, and YouTube. All of these western social media websites can be accessed without a VPN in Hong Kong, Macau, and Taiwan.

Virtual Private Networks

A Virtual Private Network (VPN) facilitates a quick, secure access to a remote server. This server allows users to connect using a connection manager profile. TESOL professionals can purchase a VPN in their home country or in China so that they may gain access to websites that are on the Ministry of Industry and Information Technology's "block list." A simple Internet search can produce several VPN companies for use on your computer and smart devices.

Chapter Ten
Mainland Banking and Finance

What You Will Learn In This Chapter:

- Mainland Banking and Finance Overview

- Major Chinese Financial Institutions

- ATM/Debit Cards

- Yuan Anatomy 101

- Sending Money via Western Union

- Wiring Money

- Money Exchange and Exchange Rates

- Money and Banking Phrases

Mainland Banking and Finance Overview

The mainland banking and finance industry is led by four (4) major state-owned commercial financial institutions: the Agricultural Bank of China (ABC), the Bank of China (BOC), China Construction Bank (CCB), and the Industrial and Commercial Bank of China (ICBC). The Chinese Government

116 Living In China

introduced a commercial banking law in 1995 that created the commercialization of these four banks and each has its own specialty. The Industrial and Commercial Bank of China is the largest bank on the China mainland and is the major supplier of funds to the country's urban areas and manufacturing sector. The Bank of China specializes in foreign-exchange transactions and trade finance. When a TESOL professional needs to exchange foreign currency into Renminbi (RMB), BOC is the financial institution responsible for completing this transaction. CCB specializes in medium to long-term credit for infrastructure projects and urban housing development while Agricultural Bank of China provides financing to China's agricultural sector usually in the form of wholesale and retail loans to farmers and town & village enterprises (TVEs).

Major Chinese Financial Institutions

Unlike major western financial institutions, Chinese banks and financial institutions are usually open 7 days a week (which includes Sunday). The reason why western financial institutions are closed a half a day on Saturday and all of Sunday is because of the religious culture where Sunday is traditionally a day of rest. Though culturally and traditionally spiritual, China is officially an atheist country so religion doesn't impact daily business.

ATM/Debit Cards

ATM/Debit Cards (with UnionPay logo)

ATM/Debit Cards in China function like their western counterparts with the exception of the financial logo at the bottom. In most western countries, there's a VISA, MasterCard, or Discover logo. China's financial institutions display a *UnionPay logo* which can be used almost anywhere in Asia. One thing to be mindful of is that this ATM/Debit card can be used in many Asian countries but cannot be used in most western countries (as of the date of this publication).

Yuan Anatomy 101

The Chinese currency is the Renminbi (yuan) and is designated by the symbol ¥ or simply by using CNY. It's also known informally as the *kuai*, like the US Dollar is informally known as the *buck*. TESOL professionals are paid in RMB and many times can have a percentage of their salary converted to another currency (usually their home country's currency). This is part of contract negotiations (*see Chapter Five, Contracts*). There are counterfeit RMB 100s throughout the country and in order to be sure that you do not become a victim of counterfeit money, the government has recently issued a new RMB 100 note that makes it much more difficult to copy. The anti-forgery features increases the likelihood that you won't become a victim of counterfeit currency. To learn more, visit http://bit.ly/1p85E4l.

Sending Money via Western Union

Many TESOL professionals send money back to their home country and one way to do this is through Western Union. In most Chinese cities, the financial institution that is responsible for conducting this transaction is the Agricultural Bank of China (ABC). Simply bring in your passport and money that you'd like to send via Western Union. A fee will be assessed which is based on the current percentage allotted for this type of transaction.

TESOL Tip	Be aware that attempting to send money via Western Union on Fridays or the last weekend of the month may be impossible because all financial institutions go through an end-of-the-month procedure. Develop a relationship with the Western Union representative and check with your local ABC branch.

Wiring Money

When there is a need to wire money, this process is a bit more complicated. The transaction is performed by China Construction Bank and TESOL professionals will need to produce their passport, current work contract with the institution certification (RED STAMP) detailing the TESOL professional's full name, passport number, dates of contractual agreement, monthly salary, contact person, and the contact person's phone number. These documents will need to be presented each time a money wire transaction is performed. The maximum amount for a money wire is 10,000 yuan (roughly $1,600 USD) per day *as of the date of this publication*.

TESOL Tip	Develop a relationship with an English-speaking Banker. Ask for their name, phone number, email, WeChat, QQ, and use them as a point of contact for all of your banking needs. Chinese bankers are very friendly and will gladly assist you.

Money and Banking Phrases

Traveling internationally requires a good understanding of many things: geography, cultures, languages, food, and so forth. However, one major thing one must understand is how money translates into goods and services for use during your travel. China has a fairly simple understanding of currency terms and phrases as are outlined in this section.

Currency Denominations

The largest Chinese currency note is the 100 RMB note. Because this is the largest note available, many times it is advisable to request paying large expenses electronically. However, many Chinese prefer to use the system of passing cash so you may have a handful of 100 RMB notes in order to pay a bill. Here's the RMB notes in descending order:

100 元 (yi bai yuan)
50 元 (wu shi yuan)
20 元 (er shi yuan)
10 元 (shi yuan)
5 元 (wu yuan)
1 元 (yi yuan)
———
5 角 (wu jiao)
1 角 (yi jiao)

TESOL Tip	For current rates, go to www.xe.com, download the XE app, or visit a local Chinese bank branch and request the current rate from your home currency.

Banking Terminology

In major Chinese cities like Beijing, Shanghai, Hong Kong, Shenzhen, and Guangzhou, many banks will have English speakers to assist you. However, smaller cities may not have the luxury of having a native English speaker there to assist you. As a result, it will be necessary for you to be able to communicate effectively with the bank representative. Here is some bank terminology that can be useful when visiting a Chinese bank:

    取钱 (qǔ qián) - to withdraw money
    银行 (yín hang) - bank
    兑换 (duì huàn) - exchange
    兑换率 (duì huàn lǜ) - exchange rate
    现金 (xiàn jīn) - cash
    欧元 (ōu yuan) - Euro (currency)
    账户 (zhàng hù) - bank account
    自动提款机 (zìdòng tíkuǎnjī) - ATM
    货币 (huòbì) - currency
    外币 (wàibì) - foreign currency
    美圆 (měiyuán) - U.S. Dollar
    结余 (jiéyú) - account balance

Useful Banking Phrases

我可以换多少？ *(wǒ kěyǐ huàn duōshǎo?)*
How much can I change?

取款机在那？ *(qǔkuǎnjī zài nǎ?)*
Where is the ATM?

今天兑换率是？ *(jīntiān duìhuànlǜ?)*
What is the exchange rate today?

我想换一千块美元。 *(wǒ xiǎng huàn yì qiān kuài měiyuán.)*
I would like to exchange $1,000.

Chapter Eleven

Housing

What You Will Learn In This Chapter:

- Leasing Agents in China

- How to Search for Housing

- Standard Fixtures in Chinese Apartments

- Landlords

- Leasing Agreements

- Rental Deposits

- Rental Examples

- Items Needed for Rental

Leasing Agents in China

Leasing an apartment in China is quite similar to leasing an apartment in western nations but there are a few idiosyncrasies involved. When preparing to lease an apartment in China, the first step to search for a suitable one. Unless you have a Chinese friend or a representative from your company assist you, you'll have to find a leasing agent. It's very easy to find a leasing agent because their offices are located downstairs in the apartment complex in which you're seeking to rent. Keep in mind that leasing agents in China get paid a commission for showing an apartment if you rent it. If you decide to not rent the apartment, no fee is required. The leasing agent's commission is usually one-half of one month's rent and this is a one-time fee. If you are asked to pay more, this may not be a suitable apartment complex in which to lease. Paying one-half of one month's rent is a standard rate countrywide.

Responsibilities for leasing agents vary according to locale, apartment complex, and so forth. Generally speaking, leasing agents are responsible for billing tenants for electricity, making sure that mail is placed in mailboxes, general maintenance of the facilities, and security. The leasing agent is a good person to know during your stay in China.

How to Search for Housing

As mentioned above, one of the best ways to search for housing is to select an apartment complex and walk directly to the front desk and ask an agent to show you an apartment. Be sure to have an idea of your price range so that you won't waste the leasing agent's time or yours. Another way to search for an apartment is to request your company to assign a representative to you. This person will be responsible to answer your questions, address your needs and concerns, and provide you with much needed guidance. Be sure to let this person know your price range, what you desire in an apartment, etc. It's usually best to let a local (native) assist you in an apartment search so that you won't be overpriced. Many times, there is a *local price* and a *foreigner price*. Your representative will know which price best suits you.

Still another to search for apartments is via leasing and *"Craigslist-type"* websites. Just remember that many times these websites are in Mandarin and you may need assistance.

Standard Fixtures in Chinese Apartments

Chinese apartments come furnished with standard fixtures. These standard fixtures include a double bed (queen size), wardrobe, curtains, air conditioning (which also doubles as a heater), TV, couch/sofa, chair, lamp or overhead lighting, sofa, coffee table, dining table, kitchen utensils (chopsticks, cutlery, spatula; no silverware), rice cooker, large wok, microwave, saucepan, hotplate and/or burners on top of the counter (there's no oven), kettle, washing machine, and Western-style toilet. Apartments will vary according to locale, city, cost of living,

Housing   *127*

Furnished Apartment Example

(this is a real apartment located in Kunming, Yunnan)

Chinese furnished apartments typically include: Bed, wardrobe, curtains, air conditioning, TV, couch/sofa, chair, lamp or overhead lighting, coffee table, dining table, kitchen utensils (chopsticks, cutlery, spatula), rice cooker, wok, microwave, shallow saucepan, washing machine, refrigerator, and Western-style toilet.

128 Living In China

and other unforeseen factors. *Remember to negotiate.*

 **TESOL Tip**: Many people feel uncomfortable with haggling but it's a significant part of Chinese culture. If you are good with haggling, then you will do well in China. If you are a bit uncomfortable with haggling, then you may find some challenges. Remember to negotiate everything!

Electrical outlets are also standard features in Chinese apartments. There are 3 distinct electrical outlets in the whole country and the outlets are labeled according to locale.

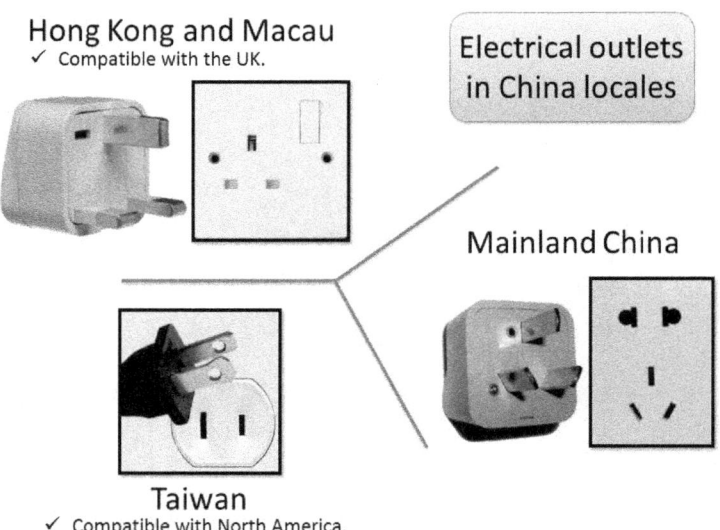

> **TESOL Tip**: When traveling frequently between Taiwan, Hong Kong, Macau, and mainland China, it's always best to keep a Universal Adapter to make finding power outlets much easier.

Landlords

Chinese landlords, in my experience, have been very friendly! Then again, I suppose anyone would be friendly if you as a foreigner paid your rent on-time. Landlords know and understand that foreigners will pay a higher-priced apartment without knowing that others in the apartment complex are paying much less. Hence, I would recommend that you have a representative with you while seeking apartments. Word to the wise: it's best to develop a strong relationship with your landlord.

Leasing Agreements

Leasing agreements in China are quite similar to those in western countries. The major difference is that many leasing agreements are written in Mandarin, only. NEVER sign a leasing agreement until it has been reviewed and discussed with your Chinese representative, the landlord, and the leasing agent present at the same time. This is standard procedure in China. Once you sign the leasing agreement, you are responsible for what's outlined in the agreement regardless if you understand it or not. Treat apartment leasing agreements as one would treat any other contract. Refer to *Chapter 5, Contracts*. Once signed, the leasing agreement should be validated with the landlord's signature, the leasing agent's signature, and a RED STAMP.

Rental Deposits

Most apartments in China require you to pay first, last, security deposit, and an agent's fee (usually one-half of one month's rent) before being given the keys to the apartment. The schedule of payment depends on the locale, city, landlord, leasing agent, and so forth. There is no one standard procedure as one might suspect because everything is negotiable. Here are two (2) examples of rental amounts and how much you'd have to pay to move into your new apartment. It is recommended that the apartment lease coincides with the TESOL professional's work contractual obligation so that there is no overlap. This should be discussed in the contract negotiations for the new apartment. For example, if your Chinese Visa expires on July 31st but the 12-month rental agreement expires on August 31st, it would be wise to bring this to the attention of the landlord and leasing agent in order to negotiate an earlier contract exit (11 months versus 12 months). This is totally acceptable as long as it's discussed beforehand. Remember to never sign a contract unless you know everything that's in it.

Rental Examples

Since rental rates vary greatly from city to city and region to region, an example for Tier 1 and Tier 2 cities is provided. Rental deposits are fairly consistent throughout mainland China.

EXAMPLE 1.
Tier 1 city basic rental rates (includes Shanghai, Shenzhen, Guangzhou, Beijing, Tianjin, Chongqing, Chengdu)

Monthly rent: 4000元 (~$644 USD)

- First month's rent: 4000元
- Last month's rent: 4000元
- Security deposit: 4000元
- Agent's fee: 2000元

TOTAL: 14000元* (~$2,250 USD)

*due at move-in

EXAMPLE 2.
Tier 2 city basic rental rates (includes Kunming, Changsha, Lanzhou, Xiamen, Fuzhou, Zhengzhou)

Monthly rent: 1500元 (~$240 USD)

- Month 1 rent: 1500元
- Month 1 rent: 1500元
- Month 1 rent: 1500元
- Month 1 rent: 1500元
- Month 1 rent: 1500元
- Month 1 rent: 1500元
- Agent's fee: 2000元

TOTAL: 9750元* (~$1,570 USD)

*due at move-in

Items Needed for Leasing

- Passport.

- Proof of Income (typically a work contract).

- Cash on-hand (credit/debit cards not accepted). Cash payment is conducted in two separate transactions on the day of move-in: 1) Pay the landlord/owner the agreed upon amount 2) Pay the leasing agent their commission. Leasing agent commissions are typically not negotiable. Obtain An invoice/receipt (发票 *fa piao*) for every transaction.

- Registration with the local police department. NOTE: some companies do this for you—you must confirm that you are registered with the local police department. If not, locate the local police department that has jurisdiction to your apartment, not your place of employment. **Failure to register with the local police department could have repercussions that affect your visa status.**

TESOL Tip	When registering with the Local Police Department, bring your Passport, employment contract, apartment lease, and be prepared to answer questions pertaining to why you're in China, your employment status, how long you plan to stay, etc.

Chapter Twelve

Grocery Stores and Restaurants

What You Will Learn In This Chapter:

- Basics of the Chinese Diet

- Grocery Store and Restaurant Overview

- Western Grocery Stores in China

- Specialty Shops, Coffee Shops, and Boutiques

- Fast Food Restaurants

Basics of the Chinese Diet

The traditional Chinese diet is a fundamental building block of Chinese culture and society. Based off of what is known today as traditional Chinese medicine (TCM), the Chinese diet has roots in the 本草纲目 (běn cǎo gāng mù). The Bencao gangmu is a comprehensive Chinese Medical Journal published in 1590 by 李时珍 (Lǐ Shízhēn) during the Ming Dynasty (1378-1644, *see Chapter Two*) that outlines uses for plants, animals, minerals, and other items believed to have medicinal properties. Each of the 1,892 entries is characterized as a *"gāng."* The Bencao gangmu is significant because the Chinese

134   Living In China

diet is viewed as "medicine" that provides sustenance, nutrition, and balance to the body. The Chinese cultural infrastructure today continues to be guided by the Bencao gangmu and is sought after by those in the west to help fight diseases such as cancer, diabetes, obesity, and other degenerative conditions.

Grocery Store and Restaurant Overview

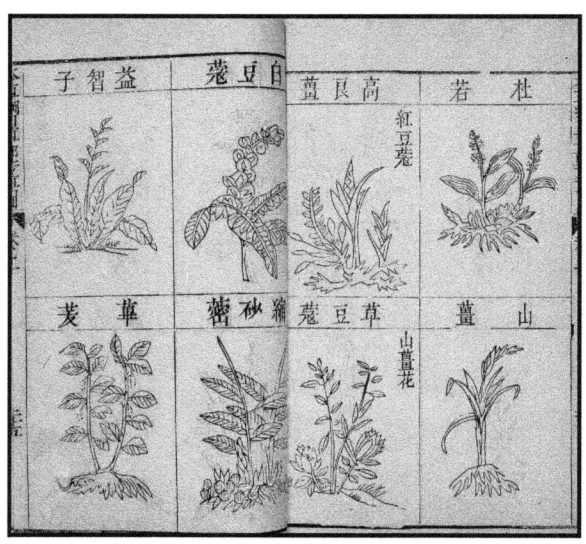

With a basic understanding of TCM and the Chinese diet, learning to understand Chinese grocery stores and restaurants should be easy. All items are fresh and usually sitting at room temperature. Meats included. The reasoning is that the food will be eaten the same day. Western grocery stores and restaurants store meats in a frozen food section. A frozen food section generally will not be found in a Chinese grocery store. Chinese grocery stores and restaurants cut meats on-the-spot and include every part of the animal being butchered. For example, if you order a fish in a restaurant, the fish is usually alive in the fish tank. You select the swimming fish, inform the waiter/waitress which one you'd like to order by pointing at it, and then the cook will grab a net and retrieve the fish. The fish is then cooked and served to you with the head attached. Food is served with the head attached to ensure that you are getting what you ordered. This can be somewhat uncomfortable for westerners but eventually it becomes commonplace. For fruits and vegetables, it is customary to weigh all items while in the fruits and vegetables section prior to checking out at the cash register.

In addition to grocery stores, there are many open markets throughout the country in every city. Open markets have fresh meats, fruits, vegetables, nuts, and other items specific to the region. In southwestern Yunnan, open markets add spices, world famous Puer tea, and cultural foods specific to the region while north central Xi'an adds country famous noodles and Muslim dishes.

Western Grocery Stores in China

Part of the cultural transition to Chinese society will include *food familiarity*. To assist in this process, several western grocery store chains are located in larger cities throughout the country. Major western grocery store chains include Vanguard, Carrefour, Walmart, SAMS, and Metro. While not perfect, you will find most foods consistent with western countries as these chains specialize in the importing of western foods. Keep in mind that if you're in a city with a large foreign population, it's likely that you'll have a higher probability of purchasing a foreign food item. If you reside in a remote area of the country, you may have to travel to larger cities like Beijing, Shanghai, Shenzhen, Chongqing, or Hong Kong in order to get that comfort food item.

Western Grocery Stores

Western and western-themed grocery stores located in various Chinese cities:

- Vanguard
- Carrefour
- Walmart
- SAM'S Club
- METRO

Specialty Shops, Coffee Shops, and Boutiques

Contemporary Chinese society is very progressive and at the cutting edge of several cultural innovations. This includes specialty shops, coffee shops, and boutiques. Traditionally found in larger metropolitan areas like Shanghai and Hong Kong, local and foreign brands are engaging the Chinese customer like never before. Starbucks, a global coffee behemoth, has shops located throughout the country and continues to grow by engaging the customer with the signature *Starbucks experience.*

Fast Food Restaurants

Right behind Starbucks are other western brands that engage the Chinese consumer. KFC is the largest and most popular fast food restaurant among Chinese consumers followed by McDonald's, Burger King, Papa John's, Pizza Hut, and Subway (not necessarily in that order). Though not true fast food in the western sense, a few Chinese fast food brands include Zhen Kungfu, Dico's, and Quanjude (Beijing-based only).

Western Fast Food

Western fast food restaurants located in various Chinese cities:

- Burger King
- McDonald's
- KFC
- Papa John's
- Pizza Hut
- Subway

Chinese Fast Food

Chinese fast food restaurants located in various Chinese cities:

- Dico's
- Zhen Kungfu (aka Real Kungfu)
- Quanjude (located in Beijing)

Chapter Thirteen
APPs for Survival

What You Will Learn In This Chapter:

- Overview of APPs for Chinese and Asian Acculturation
- Essential APPs for Cultural Transition
- Emoji for Smart Devices and Chinese Social Media

Overview of APPs for Chinese and Asian Acculturation

Mobile phone usage in China is at an incredible market penetration of 91% of 1.24 billion mobile subscribers countrywide. It is anticipated that this number will continue to rise especially with the addition of smart devices and wearables like the iPhone 6S, Xiaomi Mi4, Samsung Galaxy S6, Apple Watch, and Pebble Smartwatch. Like never before, relocation to another country and adapting to the local culture has become easier. It is also possible to learn the local language *as you go* or simply use a translator to get what you need. Smart devices have certainly changed the way that we live and living and teaching in China and visiting other Asian nations no longer needs to be intimidating to the average language learner because *there's now an app for that* to make life a bit easier.

140 Living In China

Technologically, that is.

Here's a snapshot of mobile and Internet market penetration in China. Rural China has a large mobile subscriber population because there is very little to no traditional Internet infrastructure. Therefore, many smaller towns and cities rely predominately on mobile devices and apps associated with these smart devices.

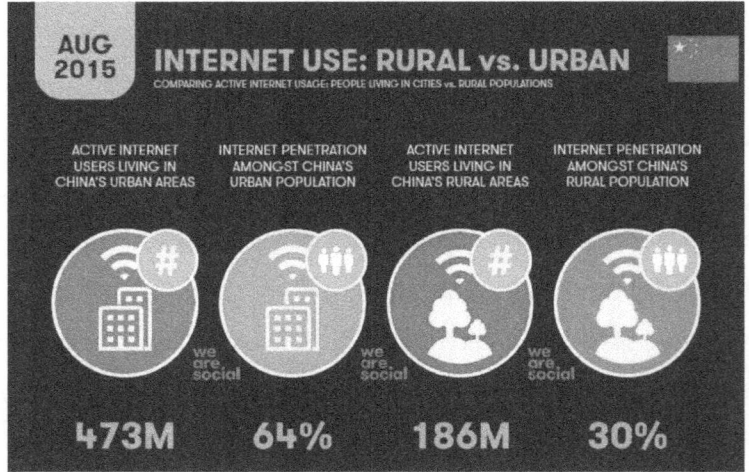

Essential APPs for Cultural Transition

There are thousands of apps out there and while some are quite useful, many are just a waste of time for the serious

APPs for Survival *141*

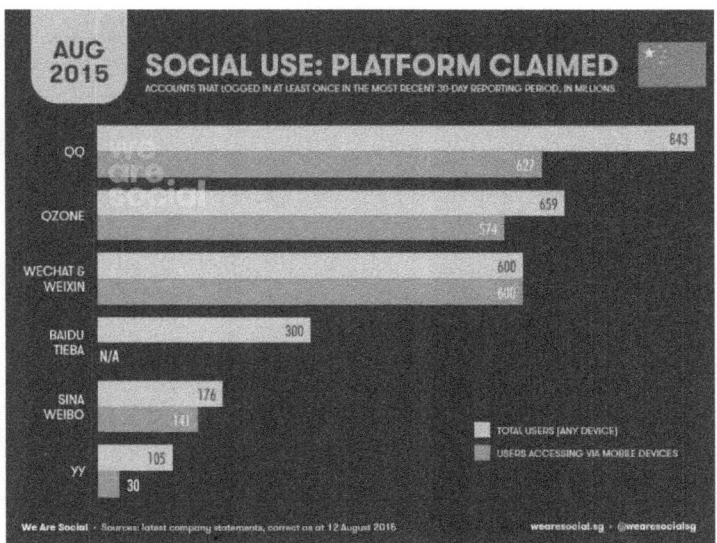

TESOL professional. Though this list isn't all inclusive, I have compiled several apps that have been useful in my cultural transition and interaction in China. I have divided these apps into the categories of Connectivity, Finance/Valuation, Social Media, Metros, Teaching, and Travel. Keep in mind that many of these apps overlap into other categories.

The top major social networks in China are QZone (Tencent QQ) at 625 million monthly active users, WeChat with 355 million active users, Sina Weibo with 129 million active users.

142 Living In China

TEACHING: Dictionary.com, Pleco, Google Translate, Action Words, Grammar Up, .Phrasalstein

FINANCE/VALUATION: Industrial and Commercial Bank of China (ICBC), Agricultural Bank of China (ABC), China Construction Bank (CCB), Pingan Bank, China Merchants Bank (CMBO, XE, Oanda.

SOCIAL MEDIA: WeChat, QQ, Youku, LinkedIn.

METROS/SUBWAYS: 24 countrywide.

CONNECTIVITY: Skype, Whatsapp, Viber, QQ, WeChat

TRAVEL: C-Trip, Qunar, Hotels.com, Trivago, Agoda

Emoji for Smart Devices and Chinese Social Media

Emoji are ideograms, smileys or "picture characters" that originated in Japanese electronic messages and webpages. Because of their popularity, they have rapidly spread outside of Japan into global culture. Emoji are often presented as pictographs—images of things such as faces, weather, vehicles and buildings, food and drink, animals and plants—or icons that represent emotions, feelings, or activities. In Chinese social media, there are specific icons used to represent aspects of Chinese culture and society. Below are some in popular social media QQ and WeChat.

144   Living In China

QQ and WeChat Emoji for smart devices

Popular Emoji

TESOL Tip	For great student interaction, use QQ and WeChat to connect outside of the classroom. Social media motivates learners to practice English in everyday life while navigating social media and new technology.

Chapter Fourteen
For Education Directors & Administrators

What You Will Learn In This Chapter:

- Establishing Relationships in China

- International Recruitment

- International University Agreements

- Major Provincial Universities

- Steps to Establishing International University Relations

Establishing Relationships in China

With a population exceeding 1 billion, China is an incredible financial and logistical opportunity by its sheer number and developing relationships with credible businesses, organizations, colleges and universities will be beneficial to anyone willing to put in hard work over time. However, major barriers such as Chinese language and culture exist. Those who connect with China rely on pursuing agents and Asian-focused divisions in order to mitigate risks while others take time to develop relationships over time. As with any relationship, there are pros and cons to each approach but ultimately each approach is dependent on the time-related goals of the business or organization. For example, western school admissions actively seek to recruit Chinese students in a shorter amount of time versus a university Asian Studies program or multinational business seeking to establish and cultivate a relationship over time. Both scenarios require understanding of Chinese language and culture.

Tips for establishing fruitful Chinese relationships:

- **Most Chinese relationships begin with a meal.** No meal, no relationship. This is cultural and Chinese have been engaging in this behavior as part of their society for thousands of years. Additionally, a welcome meal establishes a baseline for trust. Many western cultures fail miserably with this important piece of cultural etiquette.

- **Learn some basic Mandarin.** One does not have to be an expert in the language but showing that you have interest in learning is enough for many Chinese. This also reflects on your character in determining if a lasting relationship will occur.

- **Establish sincere, direct eye contact.** Chinese look directly into another's eyes when conversing and this establishes a sense of trust. In western business, it's always a good idea to look directly into another's eyes with sincerity while firmly shaking hands. This also applies to contemporary Chinese culture.

- **Discuss personal life.** Generally speaking, Chinese do not see a separation between one's personal and professional life as western cultures do. In development for thousands of years, it's highly unlikely that Chinese cultural etiquette will change overnight. Therefore, be prepared to field questions about your personal life during a face-to-face meeting when requested.

International Recruitment

TESOL opportunities in China are plentiful and in conjunction with the Ministry of Education and provincial education bureaus, salaries and English teaching jobs are plentiful. As previously mentioned, China is desperate for English-speaking TESOL professionals and salaries and benefits are comparable with this need. Many graduate student programs recruit students to teach in China as part of their curriculum.

When establishing a relationship with a Chinese school, request to work with one or two points of contact. This will ensure forging a relationship over time with administrators that are significant to your organization's needs. Many times there are *policy changes* in China (meaning that someone may no longer reside in their current role) and in order to cultivate the relationship, it's important to stay abreast of pertinent changes in the organization's personnel through consistent contact. The initial point of contact may be the public relations officer, recruiter, international affairs office, deputy director, director of studies, and so forth.

International University Agreements

Establishing university or departmental agreements with domestic universities and organizations is very detailed and takes time. International university agreements are the same but require much needed attention to detail. The Chinese university system is quite flexible and welcoming to establishing agreements with western and other foreign universities. However, it's important to recognize that every province has different needs based on the direction of China's Ministry of Education (*see Chapter Two*). This should be addressed when establishing any type of university agreement in order to create a WIN-WIN situation. For example, Yunnan Minzu University (YMU) is a key provincial university in China that caters to 25 of the 56 ethnic minority groups established by the Central Government. YMU receives certain funding for ethnic minority groups while other Chinese universities may not receive these specific funds or recruitment opportunities. This also goes for specific departments. If the School of Engineering at Peking University wants to establish a relationship with The University of Toledo, then specifics like curriculum development and student exchange may need to be addressed.

Major Provincial Universities

Major provincial universities usually have the word *"Normal"* in their university name. For example, Yunnan *Normal* University is a major university in Yunnan Province with research facilities and active domestic and foreign faculty members. However, this isn't always the case. Some also include *"Jiaotong"* in their university name such as Xi'an *Jiaotong* University. Refer to the Major Universities in the Appendix.

Steps to Establishing International University Relations

> **TESOL Tip**

- Call, Skype, or QQ (*see Chapter Fifteen*) instead of emailing when initially establishing a relationship. Chinese business culture focuses on personal relationships and sending an email without first meeting is impersonal. In fact, the email may be ignored completely. Since a foreign administrator usually isn't in China to meet in-person, calling or Skyping is the next best thing.

- Allow the Chinese institution to guide the initial contact. Most Chinese universities are excited about establishing a relationship with a foreign university so there should be a sense of trust in the initial stages of the negotiation.

- Request an overview of the university and send an overview of your university via courier.

- Address the school's unique features that interest you.

- Ask for student and/or administrator references.

- Provide insight into why you would like to develop and establish a relationship.

- Request to have one point of contact for all negotiations.

152 Living In China

- <u>Never</u> get the name of the school wrong.

- Request that all articulation agreements and memorandum of understanding documents be typewritten in both English and Mandarin and certified by a translator.

- Facilitate faculty and student exchange.

- Encourage joint research for faculty and students.

153

Networking

Relationship Management
Guanxi vs Networking
Sample Interview Questions

Chapter Fifteen
Building a Professional Network

The importance of building a professional network is essential for the serious TESOL professional. A strong professional network in China and Asia provides leverage for navigating the TESOL terrain and the English language business is huge in China. One key component in building a dynamic network is through the use of social media. The most used social media tools for TESOL professionals in China are QQ, WeChat, and LinkedIn.

Social Media

Social media generally refers to interactions among people where they create, share, and exchange information and ideas in virtual communities and networks. This method is by far one of the best ways to engage teachers, colleagues, and parents in China. According to *We Are Social,* a social media PR agency that tracks Internet usage in Asia and around the globe, China has about 653 million active social media users as of Jan 2016 (see illustration). Beijing in northern China has the highest Internet penetration in the country trending at roughly 75%.

QQ

QQ is one of the most popular Instant Messaging (IM) clients used China. From the countryside to the city, young to

Building a Professional Network **155**

old, everyone in China is familiar with QQ and uses its IM and video chat tools to communicate. With more than 710 million users worldwide, QQ provides international users access to the vast Chinese network. It's available in several languages. It also integrates useful apps ranging from newsfeeds to games and video, with more free apps you can add. Translations, currency conversions, and other essential features for travelers make QQ worth having. All of QQ's services are free. You can download the client to your mobile phone, desktop, laptop, or notebook from http://www.imqq.com. As of January 2015,

156 Networking

Tencent (QQ's parent company) reports that there are 829 million active QQ accounts with a peak of 176.4 million simultaneous online QQ users.

Building a Professional Network

WeChat

As the second largest social network in China, WeChat is quite popular with TESOL students. WeChat is a mobile text and voice messaging communication service is developed by Tencent, also the parent company of QQ. Also known as Wēixìn (微信), WeChat is the largest standalone messaging app by monthly active users. WeChat services include text messaging, hold-to-talk voice messaging, broadcast (one-to-many) messaging, , wallet, sharing of photographs and videos, and location sharing. You can download WeChat at www.wechat.com. As of August 2015, WeChat had 438 million active users with 70 million outside of China. If you would like to connect with me on WeChat, simply scan my QR code displayed here.

It is determined that the top activities used on WeChat include text messaging (92%), voice messaging (90%), use of the moments option (75%), and group chatting (62%). I tend to use WeChat like Twitter when engaging my students by reiterating classroom assignment due dates, using the moments option so that they can learn more about me, and praising students for improved speaking during class.

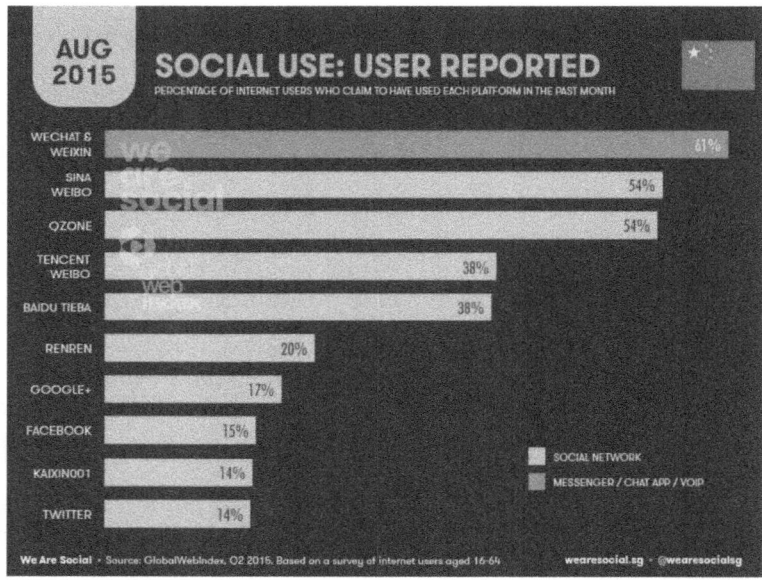

LinkedIn

LinkedIn is a business-oriented social network that is used several ways. In addition to LinkedIn connecting you with former and current colleagues, it provides strategic information on companies, business professional locations, groups and organizations, and has a global reach. For the

TESOL professional, this is ideal for career development to other areas of the globe. As of June 2013, LinkedIn boasted 259 million acquired users in more than 200 countries and territories. Available for free registration at www.linkedin.com, it has 20 available languages for the active TESOL professional. You are welcome to connect with me by going to www.linkedin.com/in/jondallas.

Relationship Management

A resource skill that is pertinent to TESOL professionals is relationship management. This is basically a strategy where you consistently and continuously engage colleagues and other professionals in your company, the community, organizational meetings, or anywhere to develop a business relationship. This is important especially in China because relationships are critical to personal and business development.

160   Networking

When engaging others in China, there are several important tips:

> **TESOL Tip**

1. *Actively network.* This is an effective career development tool where you should know your goals and ambitions when engaging other professionals.

2. *Networking should be continuous.* This means that it shouldn't be pertinent only when needing a job. If you continuously cultivate these relationships, over time you'll be able to reap the benefits of your harvest.

3. *Engage your audience.* This can occur through social media, taking someone to dinner, and so forth.

4. *Participate.* During meetings, take meaningful notes and jot down questions so that you can engage others. This shows everyone that you're listening and actively engaging.

5. *Business cards.* This method seems old and archaic in the digital age but it's still one of the most effective ways to engage others in China. Most importantly, they are relatively inexpensive and can be ordered at a local printing shop. Be sure to have your information printed in English on one side and Mandarin on the other. If you need assistance, ask a colleague.

Guanxi vs. Networking

When it comes to relationships, interactions depend on how it's viewed. For example, a personal relationship has a different *tone* than a business relationship in western culture because it tends to be more intimate. Western business relationships tend to focus solely on business and functions associated with business. The result is a shadow of a dichotomous individual that you partially understand. *Chinese culture is strikingly different.*

Developing a relationship in China requires getting to know and understand a person over a long period of time. Also, there is no separation of *personal relationship vs. business relationship* because Chinese culture and society has evolved over thousands of years from the premise that developing intimate relationships with others introduces you to their "sphere of influence." Guanxi 关系 (*guān xi*) in Chinese culture is a foundational component that refers to the basic dynamic in personalized networks of influence and have undertones that greatly overshadows the western ideas of "connections" and "relationships."

Networking

These benefits of these personalized networks of influence usually extend to extended family, colleagues, classmates, and members of common clubs or organizations and reciprocal favors are the key factor to maintaining one's influence. It is customary for Chinese to cultivate relationships in this manner and these relationships can sometimes expand in a large number of directions that includes lifelong relationships. Key observations of Guanxi include:

1. Staying in contact with members of your network is not necessary in order to bind reciprocal obligations.
2. The more you ask of someone the more you owe them.
3. Guanxi can perpetuate a never ending cycle of favors.
4. Failure to reciprocate is considered an unforgivable offense.

By comparison, western networking seems quite shallow. Networking is establishing and maintaining informal relationships with people whose acquaintance or friendship could bring advantages such as a job or other business opportunities. The major difference is that western networking has no deep *intimate component* that binds the relationship for a long period of time.

Building a Professional Network   *163*

This is a major challenge for westerners attempting to conduct business in China and for both cultures attempting to create an atmosphere of cultural understanding between the east and the west 中西文化交汇 (*zhōng xī wén huà jiāo huì*). Understanding the concept of Guanxi and networking is necessary for TESOL professionals because Chinese students and colleagues are intimately aware of this concept. As the TESOL professional, you are the outsider that needs to be able to understand classroom dynamics instead of the western perspective where it's the students that need to understand the teacher. Most Chinese classrooms will have a student leader or monitor. Get to know this individual and develop a relationship with him/her. Once this relationship is established, then you will be able to cope much better with your classroom management.

Sample Interview Questions

Asking interview questions is important because it accomplishes two goals: it expresses your interest in the position and it allows you to gain a better understanding of the company. Remember, you are interviewing the TESOL institution just as much as the institution is interviewing you.

164 Networking

This also goes for negotiating a contract (*see Chapter Five*).

I have divided potential interview questions into five major sections that apply to teaching positions in China: (1) Teaching Position, (2) Classroom Management, (3) Training and Development, (4) Salary, and (5) Relocation/Housing.

Teaching Position

- Please describe the position.
- Why is this position vacant?
- What is the start date for the position?
- What is the job description for this position?
- What benefits are associated with this position?
- What are the expectations of the successful candidate?
- When is the candidate expected to arrive in China for training?
- May I have a reference for a previous teacher in this role?

Classroom Management

- Is there already a curriculum provided or do teachers need to create lesson plans and gather teaching materials?

- Are teachers required to construct their own syllabus and/or teaching plan?

- What is or will be the average number of students per class?

- For evaluative purposes, who is the immediate/direct leader (supervisor)?

- What are expectations for teachers in the classroom?

- What criteria will be used for teacher evaluation? How often?

- How do teachers know that they've met their goals?

Training and Development

- What professional development options are available to help improve my teaching development process?

- Who can assist me with teacher development?

- What are some extracurricular activities that teachers can facilitate?

- What advancement opportunities are available?

- Will the company help compensate costs of candidates pursuing an additional teaching certification?

Networking

Salary

- What is the monthly salary increase for teachers with additional experience?
- How much is the company seeking to pay *the best* candidate?
- What other benefits are associated with this position?
- What is the rate for additional courses taught?
- What is the overtime rate?
- What is the salary amount paid during winter and spring breaks?
- Is this paid in a lump sum or on a regular schedule?
- Is it possible to pursue part-time teaching opportunities?
- Is there an end-of-contract bonus? If so, what is the amount?

Relocation/Housing

- What is the peak amount provided for relocation assistance?
- Is housing provided as an on-campus option?
- What is the amount available for housing assistance?
- What date will *Z-visa reimbursement* be processed?
- What date will the *airfare to China reimbursement* be processed?

Building a Professional Network

> **TESOL Tip**
>
> Seek opportunities to diversify your teaching credentials by adding a specialty to make yourself more attractive for your next assignment. Some TESOL specialties include teaching children, university, ethnic students, medical, IELTS, Gao Kao, and public speaking.

Appendix of Resources

2014 Chinese University Rankings

China's Dynasties

Chinese Embassies & Consulates

Chinese Ethnic Minorities

Chinese Food Basics

Chinese National Anthem

Chinese Public Holidays

City Metro/Subway Maps

Cultural Transition Stages

Essential Mandarin

Ethnic Festivals & Holidays

Major TESOL Companies

News & Media Resources

Phonemic Chart

2014 Chinese University Rankings -- Top 25

	University	City
1	Peking University	Beijing
2	Tsinghua University	Beijing
3	Shanghai Jiaotong University	Shanghai
4	Fudan University	Shanghai
5	Nanjing University	Nanjing
6	Xi'an Jiaotong University	Xi'an
7	University of Science and Technology of China	Hefei
8	Zhejiang University	Hangzhou
9	Xiamen University	Xiamen
10	Renmin University of China	Beijing
11	Wuhan University	Wuhan
12	Tongji University	Shanghai
13	Jilin University	Changchun
14	Huazhong University of Science and Technology	Wuhan
15	Northeast Normal University	Changchun
16	Beijing Normal University	Beijing
17	East China Normal University	Shanghai
18	Nankai University	Tianjin
19	Southeast University	Nanjing
20	Mudanjiang Medical College	Mudanjiang
21	Shandong University	Jinan
22	Tianjin University	Tianjin
23	South China Normal University	Guangzhou
24	Harbin Institute of Technology	Harbin
25	Nanjing Normal University	Nanjing

China's Dynasties

"The Dynasties Song"

This "Dynasties Song," sung to the tune of "Frère Jacques," can help students remember the major Chinese dynasties in chronological order.

Shang, Zhou, Qin, Han

Shang, Zhou, Qin, Han

Sui, Tang, Song

Sui, Tang, Song

Yuan, Ming, Qing, Republic

Yuan, Ming, Qing, Republic

Mao Zedong

Mao Zedong

— Courtesy of the teachers on the College Board AP-World History Listserv

Chinese Embassies & Consulates

Visa fees for standard service:

Number of Entries	U.K. Citizens	U.S. Citizens	Citizens of other countries
Single entry	£30	£90 ($140 USD)	£20 ($30USD)
Double entries	£45	£90 ($140 USD)	£30 ($45USD)
Multiple entries for 6 months	£90	£90 ($140 USD)	£40 ($60USD)
Multiple entries for 12 months or more than one year	£180	£90 ($140 USD)	£60 ($90USD)

Australia 澳大利亚

Embassy of the People's Republic of China in Australia
Ambassador Ma Zhaoxu
Contact Information:
http://au.china-embassy.org/eng/
15 Coronation Drive, Yarralumla, ACT 2600
Tel: 0061-2-6228 3999   Fax: 0061-2-6228 3990
Email: chinaemb_au@mfa.gov.cn
http://au.china-embassy.org/eng/ls/vfc/

NOTE: The Chinese Embassy and Consulates General in Australia do not accept visa applications of ordinary passport holders directly. All applicants holding ordinary passports are required to submit their visa applications to the Chinese Visa Application Service Centres located in Canberra, Sydney, Melbourne, Perth, or Brisbane according to their service areas. Post addresses are for mail applications only.

Brisbane Consulate General | Consulate General

http://www.visaforchina.org/BNE_EN/

Contact Information:

Consulate General of the People's Republic of China in Brisbane

VISA Office: Part Level 4, 140 Ann Street, Brisbane, QLD 4000, Australia

PO Box: 12545 George Street, Brisbane, QLD 4003

Tel: +61-7-3031-6300   Fax: +61-7-3221-9388

Email: bnecenter@visaforchina.org

Service Areas: QLD

Canberra Consulate General | Consulate General

http://www.visaforchina.org/CBR_EN/

Contact Information:

Consulate General of the People's Republic of China in Canberra

VISA Office: Suite201,level 2,Canberra House,40 Marcus Clarke St, Canberra, ACT 2600

P.O. Box 1862,Canberra, ACT 2601

Tel: 02 6279 7800   Fax: 02 6247 2888

Email: canberracenter@visaforchina.org

Service Areas: ACT, SA, NT

Melbourne Consulate General | Consulate General

http://www.visaforchina.org/MEL_EN/

Contact Information:

Consulate General of the People's Republic of China in Melbourne

VISA Office: Ground Floor, 570 ST.Kilda Road, Melbourne, VIC 3004, Australia

PO Box: P.O.Box 7227, Melbourne, VIC 3004

Tel: +61-03-9937-2308   Fax : +61-03-9937-2337 +61-3-9937-2338

Email: melcenter@visaforchina.org

Service Areas: VIC, TAS

Perth Consulate General | Consulate General

http://www.visaforchina.org/PER_EN/

Contact Information:

Consulate General of the People's Republic of China in Perth

VISA Office: Ground Floor, 256 Adelaide Terrace, Perth WA 6000 (Entrance via Victoria Ave)

P.O. Box 3090, East Perth, WA 6892 (Postal application only)

Tel: 08 9220 3800   Fax: 08 9221 1888

Email: perthcenter@visaforchina.org

Service Areas: WA

Sydney Consulate General | Consulate General

http://www.visaforchina.org/SYD_EN/

Contact Information:

Consulate General of the People's Republic of China in Sydney

VISA Office: Level 5, 299 Elizabeth Street, Sydney, NSW 2000, Australia.
P.O. Box 20516 World Square, Sydney, NSW 2002(mail application only)

Tel:+61-2-94758800 Fax:+61-2-92612088

Email: sydcenter@visaforchina.org

Service Areas: NSW

Canada 加国

Embassy of the People's Republic of China in Canada

Ambassador Luo Zhaohui

Contact Information:

Embassy of the People's Republic of China in Canada

http://ca.china-embassy.org/eng/

VISA Office: 515 St. Patrick Street, Ottawa, K1N 5H3

Tel: 613-789-3434 x232 (3:30pm-5:30pm by operator, during the rest of the day by auto-attendant)

Fax: 613-789-1414

E-mail: zj_uk@mfa.gov.cn

Provinces served: Ottawa Region, Newfoundland & Labrador, Nova Scotia, Prince Edward Island, Nunavut.

Calgary Consulate General | Consulate General Wang Xinping

http://calgary.china-consulate.org/eng/

Contact Information:

Consulate General of the People's Republic of China in Calgary

VISA Office: Suite 200 Century Park Place, 855-8th Ave SW, Calgary, Alberta T2P3P1

Tel: 403-930-2288 Fax: 403-699-9776

Email: chinaconsul_cal_ca@mfa.gov.cn

Provinces served: Alberta, Saskatchewan, Northwest Territories.

Montreal Consulate General | Consulate General Jiangping Zhao

http://montreal.chineseconsulate.org/fra/

Contact Information:

Consulate General of the People's Republic of China in Montreal

VISA Office: 2001 University Street, Suite 1550, Montreal, Quebec H3A2A6

Tel: 514-419-6748   Fax: 514-878-9692

Email: consulate_mtl@mfa.gov.cn

Provinces served: Quebec, New Brunswick.

Toronto Consulate General | Consulate General Fang Li

http://toronto.china-consulate.org/eng/

Contact Information:

Consulate General of the People's Republic of China in Toronto

VISA Office: 240 St. George Street, Toronto, M5R2N5   416-964-8861 Fax: 416-324-9010

Email: torontovisaoffice@gmail.com

Provinces served: Ontario, Manitoba.

Vancouver Consulate General | Consulate General Liu Fei

http://vancouver.china-consulate.org/eng/

Contact Information:

Consulate General of the People's Republic of China in Vancouver

VISA Office: 200A-1595 West Broadway, Vancouver, BC V6H3K3

Tel: 604-734-7492 778-383-2637 (15:00-17:00, M-F)   Fax: 604-734-0311

Email: visa@chinaconsulatevan.org

Provinces served: British Columbia, Yukon Territory.

New Zealand 新西兰

Embassy of the People's Republic of China in New Zealand

Ambassador Wang Lutong

http://www.chinaembassy.org.nz/eng/

Contact Information:

Embassy of the People's Republic of China in Wellington

www.chinaembassy.org.nz

2-6 Glenmore Street, Kelburn, Wellington

Tel: 04 474 9631, 04 473 3514   Fax: 04 474 9632

Email: nzchinaembassy@sina.cn

Regions served: Bay of Plenty, Gisborne, Hawke's Bay, Taranaki, Manawatu-Wanganui, Wellington

Auckland Consulate General | Consulate General Niu Qingbao

http://www.chinaconsulate.org.nz/eng/

Contact Information:

Consulate General of the People's Republic of China in Auckland

VISA Office: 630 Great South Road, Greenland, Auckland

Tel: 09 5265680, 09 5793080   Fax: 09 579 4288

Email: chinaconsul_ak_nz@mfa.gov.cn

Regions served: Northland, Auckland, Waikato

Christchurch Consulate General | Consulate General Jin Zhijian

http://christchurch.chineseconsulate.org/eng/

Contact Information:

Consulate General of the People's Republic of China in Christchurch

VISA Office: 106 Hansons Lane, Upper Riccarton, Christchurch

Tel: 03 3433650   Fax: 03 3433647

Email: consulate_chc@mfa.gov.cn

Regions served: Tasman, Nelson, Marlborough, West Coast, Canterbury, Otago, Southland

South Africa 南非

Embassy of the People's Republic of China in the Republic of South Africa

Ambassador TIAN Xuejun

http://www.chinese-embassy.org.za/eng/

Contact Information:

Embassy of the People's Republic of China in Pretoria

225 Athlone Street, Acadia 0083, Pretoria

Tel: 012-4316500,ext.6537(visa)6531,6532,6533(consular)

Fax: 012-4307620

E-mail: visa@chinese-embassy.org.za

Visa Office Hours: 08:30-12:00, Monday to Friday

E-mail: chinaconsul_ct_za@mfa.gov.cn

Capetown Consulate General | Consulate General Liang Shugen
Contact Information:
Consulate General of the People's Republic of China in Capetown
http://capetown.china-consulate.org/
25 Rhodes Avenue, Newland7700, Cape Town
Tel: 021-6740579   Fax: 021-6740583
E-mail: chinaconsul_ct_za@mfa.gov.cn

Durban Consulate General | Consulate General Diao Mingsheng
Contact Information:
Consulate General of the People's Republic of China in Durban
http://durban.china-consulate.org/eng/
45 Stirling Crescent, Durban North, Durban 4051
Tel: 031-5634534   Fax: 031-5634827
E-mail: chinaconsul_db_za@mfa.gov.cn

Johannesburg Consulate General | Consulate General Sun Dali
Contact Information:
Consulate General of the People's Republic of China in Johannesburg
http://johannesburg.china-consulate.org
25 Cleveland Road, Sandhurst, Sandton Johannesburg
Tel: 011-6857540,ext.7561,7562 Fax: 011-8835274
E-mail: chinaconsul_jb_za@mfa.gov.cn

United Kingdom 联合王国

Embassy of the People's Republic of China in the United Kingdom of Great Britain and Northern Ireland

Ambassador Liu Xiaoming

Contact Information:

Embassy of the People's Republic of China in the United Kingdom of Great Britain and Northern Ireland

http://www.chinese-embassy.org.uk/eng/

VISA Office: 31 Portland Place, London,W1B 1QD,London,W1B 1QD

Tel: 020-7631 1430 (09:00am-12:00 noon and 2:00pm-4:00pm by operator, during the rest of the day by auto-attendant)

Fax: 020 -7636 9056

E-mail: zj_uk@mfa.gov.cn

http://www.chinese-embassy.org.uk/eng/visa/

China Visa Service Application Center:

http://www.visaforchina.org/

United States 美利坚合众国

Embassy of the People's Republic of China in Washington, DC

Ambassador Cui Tiankai

Contact Information:

Embassy of the People's Republic of China in Washington, DC

http://www.china-embassy.org/eng/

VISA Office: 2201 Wisconsin Ave, N.W. Suite 110, Washington, D.C. 20007

Telephone: (202) 337-1956

Fax: (202) 588-9760

Email: visa_us@mfa.gov.cn

States served: Washington, DC, Delaware, Idaho, Kentucky, Maryland, Montana, Nebraska, North Carolina, North Dakota, South Carolina, South Dakota, Tennessee, Utah, Virginia, West Virginia, Wyoming.

New York Consulate General | Consulate General Sun Guoxiang

Contact Information:

Consulate General of the People's Republic of China in New York

http://newyork.china-consulate.org/eng/

VISA Office: 520 12th Avenue, New York, NY 10036

Tel: 212-2449392 / 212-2449456

States served: Connecticut, Maine, Massachusetts, New Hampshire, New Jersey, New York, Ohio, Pennsylvania, Rhode Island, Vermont.

Los Angeles Consulate General | Consulate General Liu Jian

Contact Information:

Consulate General of the People's Republic of China in Los Angeles

http://losangeles.china-consulate.org/eng/

VISA Office: 3rd Floor, 500 Shatto Place, Los Angeles, CA 90020

States served: Arizona, Southern California, Hawaii, New Mexico, Pacific Islands.

San Francisco Consulate General | Consulate General Yuan Nansheng

Contact Information:

Consulate General of the People's Republic of China in San Francisco

Email: visa.sf@gmail.com

Facebook: https://www.facebook.com/chineseconsulatesf

http://www.chinaconsulatesf.org/eng/

VISA Office: 415-852-5941, Fax: 415-852-5940

States served: Alaska, Northern California, Nevada, Oregon, Washington.

Chicago Consulate General | Consulate General Zhao Weiping

Contact Information:

Consulate General of the People's Republic of China in Chicago

http://www.chinaconsulatechicago.org/eng/

VISA Office: 1 East Erie St, Suite 500, Chicago, IL 60611 312-453-0210 Fax: 312-453-0211

Email: chinavisachicago@gmail.com

(send inquiries about Visa Affairs to chinavisachicago@gmail.com)

States served: Colorado, Illinois, Indiana, Iowa, Kansas, Michigan, Minnesota, Missouri, Wisconsin.

Houston Consulate General | Consulate General Li Qiangmin

Contact Information:

Consulate General of the People's Republic of China in Houston

http://houston.china-consulate.org/eng/

VISA Office: (Automatic voice):713-521-7495 (fax): 713-521-0237

Email: visahouston@hotmail.com

States served: Alabama, Arkansas, Florida, Georgia, Louisiana, Mississippi, Oklahoma, Texas.

Chinese Ethnic Minorities

Recognized Chinese Ethnic Minority Groups		
Romantization	Pinyin	中文
Han	Hàn Zú	汉族
Zhuang	Zhuàng Zú	壮族
Hui	Huí Zú	回族
Manchu	Mǎn Zú	满族
Uyghur	Wéiwú'ěr Zú	维吾尔族
Miao	Miáo Zú	苗族
Yi	Yí Zú	彝族
Tujia	Tǔjiā Zú	土家族
Tibetan	Zàng Zú	藏族
Mongol	Měnggǔ Zú	蒙古族
Dong	Dòng Zú	侗族
Bouyei	Bùyī Zú	布依族
Yao	Yáo Zú	瑶族
Bai	Bái Zú	白族
Korean	Cháoxiǎn Zú	朝鲜族
Hani	Hāní Zú	哈尼族
Li	Lí Zú	黎族
Kazakh	Hāsàkè Zú	哈萨克族

Recognized Chinese Ethnic Minority Groups		
Romantization	Pinyin	中文
Dai	Dǎi Zú	傣族
She	Shē Zú	畲族
Lisu	Lìsù Zú	傈僳族
Dongxiang	Dōngxiāng Zú	东乡族
Gelao	Gēlǎo Zú	仡佬族
Lahu	Lāhù Zú	拉祜族
Wa	Wǎ Zú	佤族
Sui	Shuǐ Zú	水族
Nakhi	Nàxī Zú	纳西族
Qiang	Qiāng Zú	羌族
Tu	Tǔ Zú	土族
Mulao	Mùlǎo Zú	仫佬族
Xibe	Xībó Zú	锡伯族
Kyrgyz	Kē'ěrkèzī Zú	柯尔克孜族
Jingpo	Jǐngpō Zú	景颇族
Daur	Dáwò'ěr Zú	达斡尔族
Salar	Sālā Zú	撒拉族
Blang	Bùlǎng Zú	布朗族
Maonan	Máonán Zú	毛南族
Tajik	Tǎjíkè Zú	塔吉克族
Pumi	Pǔmǐ Zú	普米族

Recognized Chinese Ethnic Minority Groups		
Romantization	Pinyin	中文
Achang	Āchāng Zú	阿昌族
Nu	Nù Zú	怒族
Ewenki	Èwēnkè Zú	鄂温克族
Gin	Jīng Zú	京族
Jino	Jīnuò Zú	基诺族
De'ang	Dé'áng Zú	德昂族
Bonan	Bǎo'ān Zú	保安族
Russian	Éluósī Zú	俄罗斯族
Yugur	Yùgù Zú	裕固族
Uzbek	Wūzībiékè Zú	乌孜别克族
Monba	Ménbā Zú	门巴族
Oroqen	Èlúnchūn Zú	鄂伦春族
Derung	Dúlóng Zú	独龙族
Hezhen	Hèzhé Zú	赫哲族
Gaoshan	Gāoshān Zú	高山族
Lhoba	Luòbā Zú	珞巴族
Tatars	Tǎtǎ'ěr Zú	塔塔尔族
Undistinguished	Wèi Shìbié Mínzú	未识别民族
Naturalized Citizen	Wàiguórén Jiārù Zhōngguójí	外国人加入中国籍

Chinese National Anthem

国歌 Guó Gē (March of the Volunteers)

qǐ lai   bú yuan   zuò   nú lì   de   rén men
起来！ 不 愿 做 奴隶 的 人们！
Arise! All who refuse to be slaves!

bǎ   wǒ men   de   xuè ròu,   zhù   chéng   wǒ men   xīn   de cháng chéng!
把 我们 的 血肉， 筑 成 我们 新 的 长城！
Let our flesh and blood become our new Great Wall!

Zhōng huá   mín zú   dào   le   zuì   wēi xiǎn   de   shí hòu,
中华 民族 到 了 最 危险 的 时候
As the Chinese nation faces its greatest peril,

| měi | gè | rén | bèi pò | zhe | fā chū | zuì hòu | de | hǒu sheng. |

每 个 人 被迫 着 发出 最后 的 吼声.

All forcefully expend their last cries.

| qǐ lai! | qǐ lai! | qǐ lai! |

起来! 起来! 起来!

Arise! Arise! Arise!

| wǒ men | wàn zhòng yī xīn |

我们 万众一心

Million hearts as one,

| mào | zhe | dí rén | de | pào huǒ | qián jìn! |

冒 着 敌人 的 炮火 前进!

Brave the enemy's fire, March on!

mào zhe dí rén de pào huǒ qián jìn!

冒　　着　　敌人　　的　　炮火　　前进!

Brave the enemy's fire, March on!

qián jìn!　qián jìn!　jìn!

前进!　前进!　进!

March on! March on! On!

Chinese Numbers

1	2	3	4	5	6	7	8	9	10
yi	er	san	si	wu	liu	qi	ba	jiu	shi
一	二	三	四	五	六	七	八	九	十

11	12	13	14	15	16	17	18	19	20
shi yi	shi er	shi san	shi si	shi wu	shi liu	shi qi	shi ba	shi jiu	er shi
十一	十二	十三	十四	十五	十六	十七	十八	十九	二十

90	100	1000	10 000	100 000	1 000 000
jiu shi	yi bai	yi qi-an	wan	yi wan	bai wan
九十	一百	一千	万	一万	百万

Chinese Public Holidays

Major Public Holidays 2017/18				
Name	中文	Date	2017	2018
New Year's Day	元旦	Jan 1	Dec 31 - Jan 2 off	Dec 30 - Jan 1 off
Spring Festival (Chinese New Year)	春节	Determined by Lunar calendar	Jan 27 - Feb 7 off	Feb 15 - 21 off
Lantern Festival	上元节, 元宵节	Determined by Lunar calendar	Feb 11	Mar 2
Qingming Festival (Ancestry Memorial Day)	清明节	Apr 4 or 5	Apr 4 (Apr 2-4 off)	Apr 5 (Apr 5-7 off)
May Day (Labour Day)	劳动节	May 1	Apr 29 - May 1 off	Apr 29 - May 1 off
Dragon Boat Festival	端午节	5th day of 5th Lunar month	May 30 (May 28-30 off)	Jun 18 (Jun 16-18 off)
Mid-Autumn Festival	中秋节	Aug 15 of Lunar calendar	Oct 4	Sep 24 (Sep 22-24 off)
National Day	国庆节	Oct 1	Oct 1-7 (goes until Oct 8)	Oct 1-7
Chongyang Festival	重阳节	9th day of 9th Lunar month	Oct 28 off	Oct 17 off

Other Public Holidays 2017/18				
Name	中文	Date	2017	2018
Women's Day	国际妇女节	Mar 8	half day off	half day off
Arbor Day	植树节	Mar 12	no day off	no day off
Youth Day	青年节	May 4	half day off	half day off
International Nurse Day	国际护士节	May 12	no day off	no day off
Children's Day	六一儿童节	Jun 1	day off for children under 13	day off for children under 13
CPC Founding Day	建党节	Jul 1	no day off	no day off
Army Day	建军节	Aug 1	half day off	half day off
Chinese Valentine's Day	七夕	7th day of 7th Lunar month	no day off	no day off
Victory Over Japan Day*	抗日战争胜	3-Sep	no day off	no day off
Teacher's Day	教师节	Sep 10	no day off	no day off
Memorial Day*	为烈士纪念	Sep 30	no day off	no day off
Journalist's Day	是记者节	Nov 8	no day off	no day off
Nanking Massacre Memorial Day*	南华早报	Dec 13	no day off	no day off

* Newly established holiday in 2014

City Metro/Subway Maps

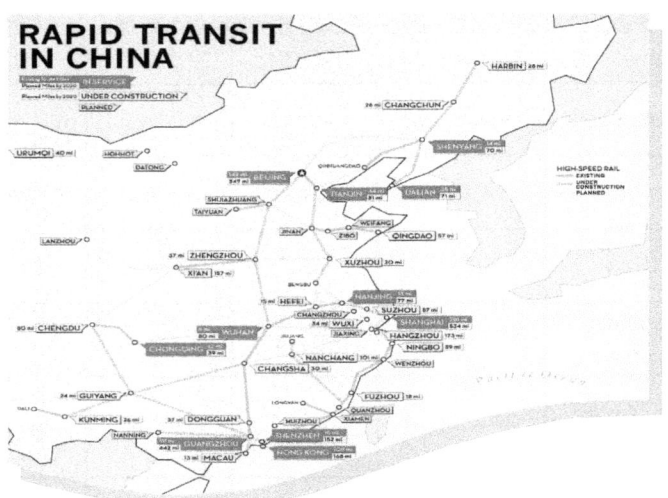

Beijing • Changchun • Changsha • Chengdu • Chongqing • Dalian • Guangzhou
Hangzhou • Harbin • Hong Kong • Kaohsiung • Kunming • Nanjing • Ningbo • Shanghai
Shenzhen • Shenyang • Suzhou • Taipei • Tianjin • Wuhan • Wuxi • Xian • Zhengzhou

BEIJING 北京

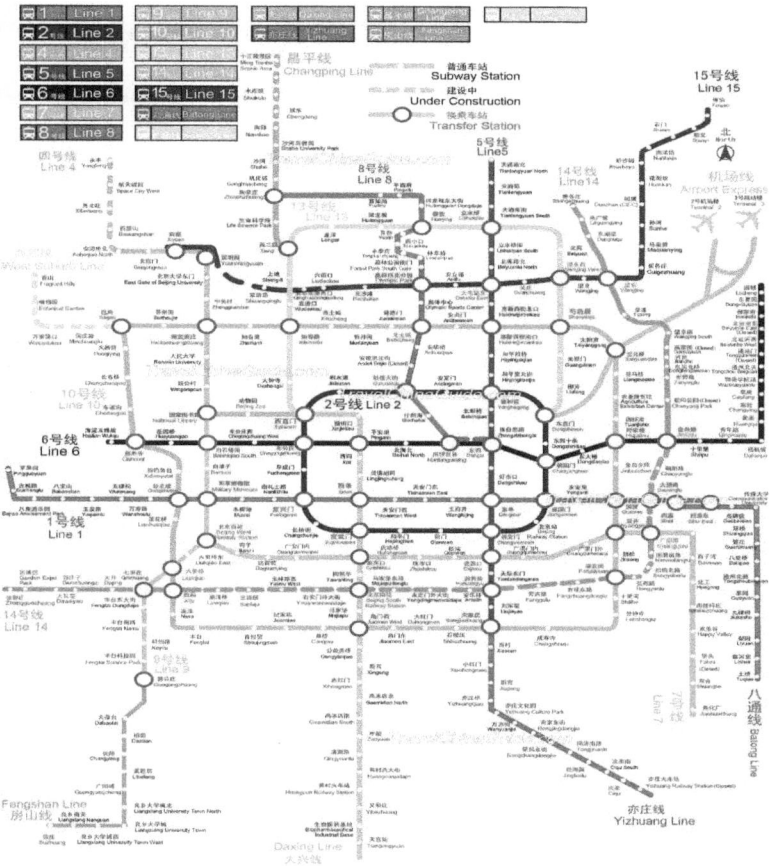

Beijing Subway Map (Click to enlarge)

长春
CHANGCHUN

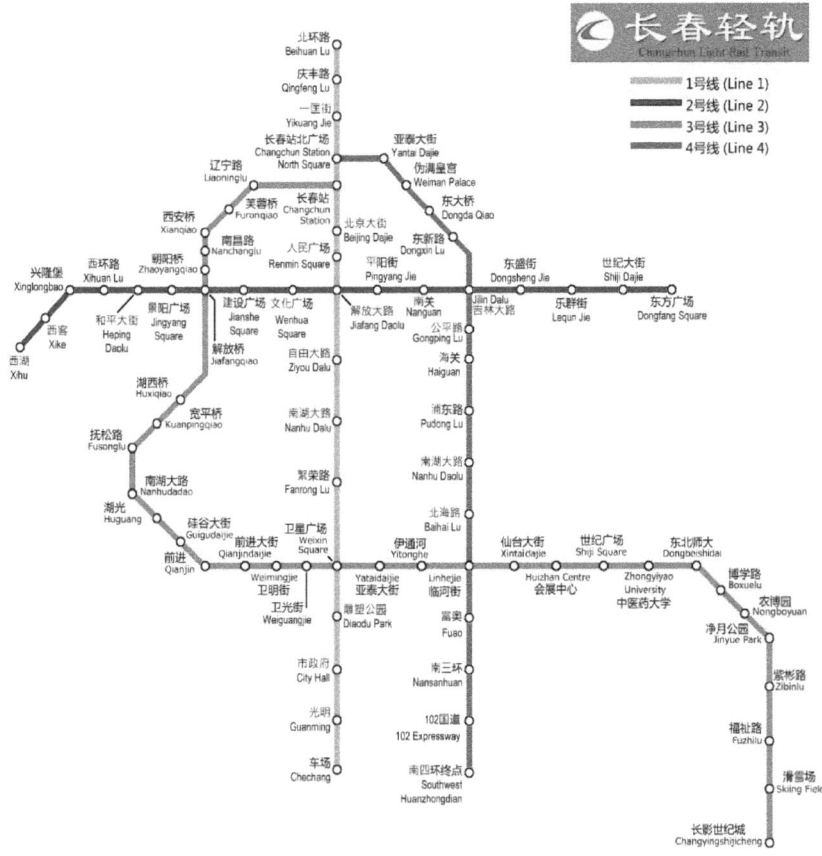

CHANGSHA

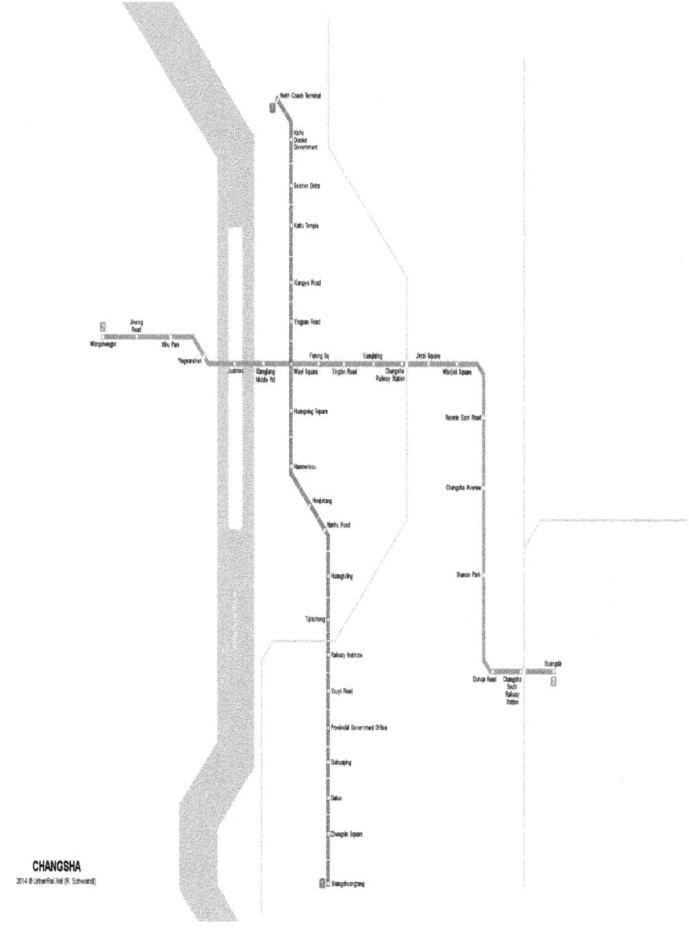

CHENGDU 成都

重庆
CHONGQING

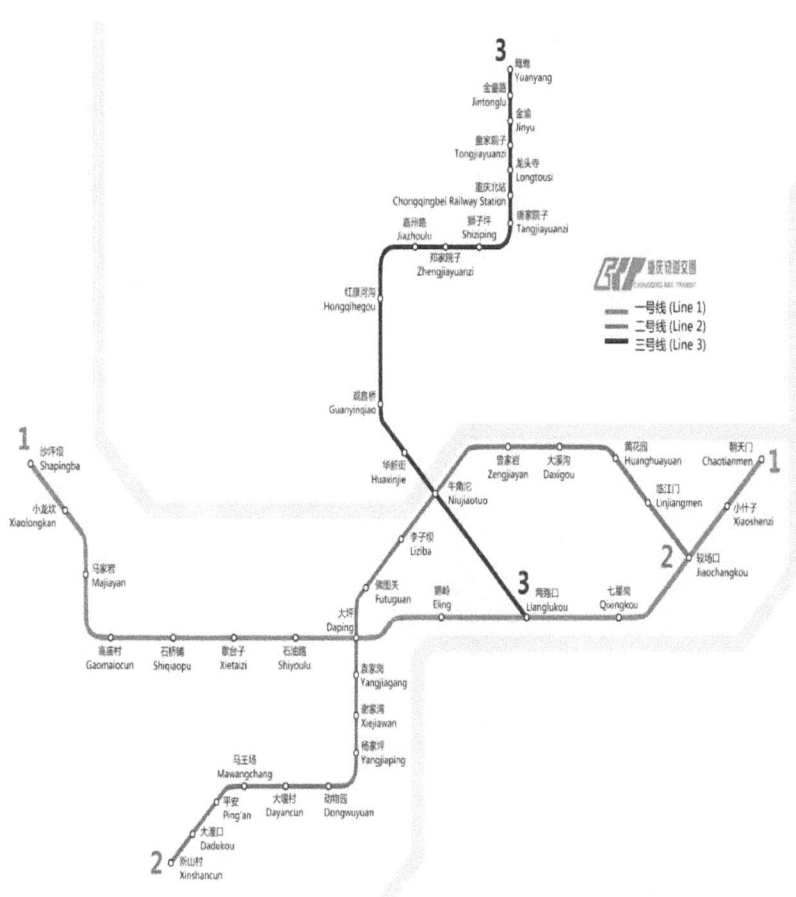

DALIAN

大连

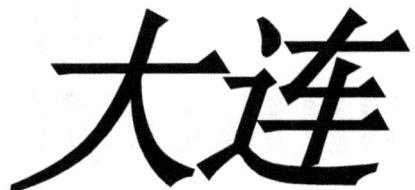

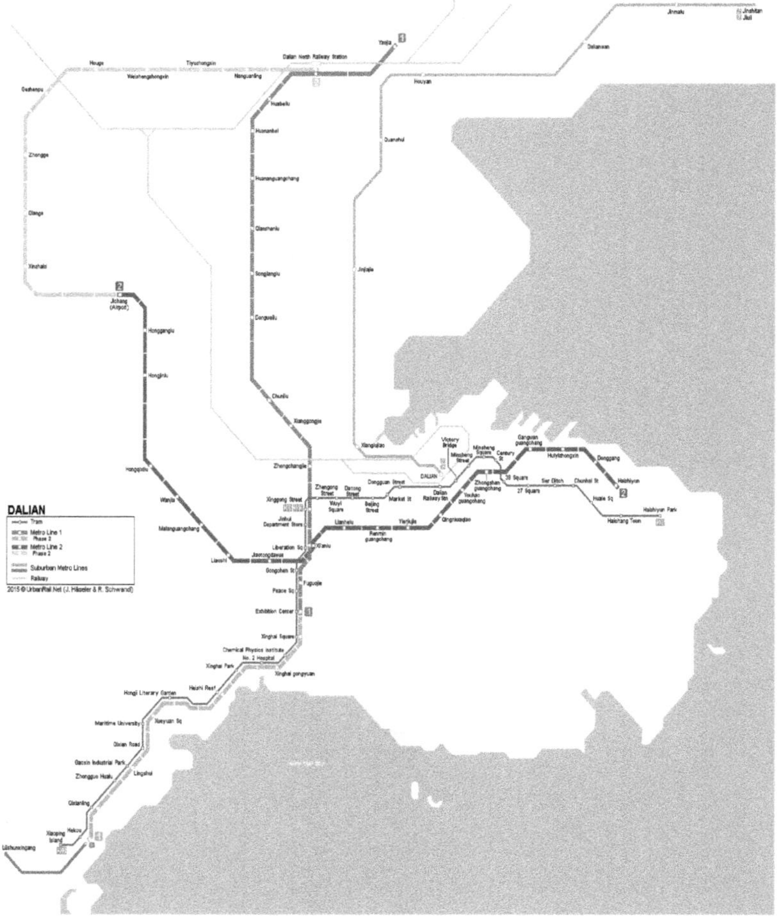
DALIAN
Tram
Metro Line 1
Phase 2
Metro Line 2
Phase 2
Suburban Metro Lines
Railway
2015 © UrbanRail.Net (J. Häseler & R. Schwandl)
Jinmalu
Jinshitan
Jiuli
Dalianwan
Yaojia
Houge
Tiyuzhongxin
Dalian North Railway Station
Weishengzhongxin
Nanguanling
Gezhenpu
Houyan
Huabeilu
Huananbei
Quanshui
Zhongge
Huananguangchang
Xinzhaizi
Jinjiajie
Jichang (Airport)
Honggangiu
Hongjinlu
Dongweilu
Songjianglu
Chunliu
Xianggongjie
Xiangluijiao
Victory Bridge
Minsheng Square
Ganguan guangchang
Century St
Huiyizhongxin
Donggang
Zhongchanglie
Dongguan Street
DALIAN
Zhongshan guangchang
38 Square
Sier Ditch
Chunhai St
Haizhiyun
Hongqixilu
Zhengong Street
Datong Street
Market St
Dalian Railway Stn
Youhao guangchang
27 Square
Huale Sq
Xinggong Street
Wuyi Square
Beijing Street
Haizhiyun Park
Haichang Town
Wanjia
Jinhui Department Store
Lianhelu
Renmin guangchang
Yierjiujie
Qingniwaqiao
Malanguangchang
Liberation Sq
Xi'anlu
Liaoshi
Jiaotongdaxue
Gongchen St
Fuguojie
Peace Sq
Exhibition Center
Xinghai Square
Chemical Physics Institute
No. 2 Hospital
Xinghai Park
Xinghai gongyuan
Heishi Reef
Hongji Literary Garden
Maritime University
Xueyuan Sq
Qixian Road
Gaoxin Industrial Park
Lingshui
Zhongguo Hualu
Qixianling
Hekou
Xiaoping Island
Lüshunxingang

广州
GUANGZHOU

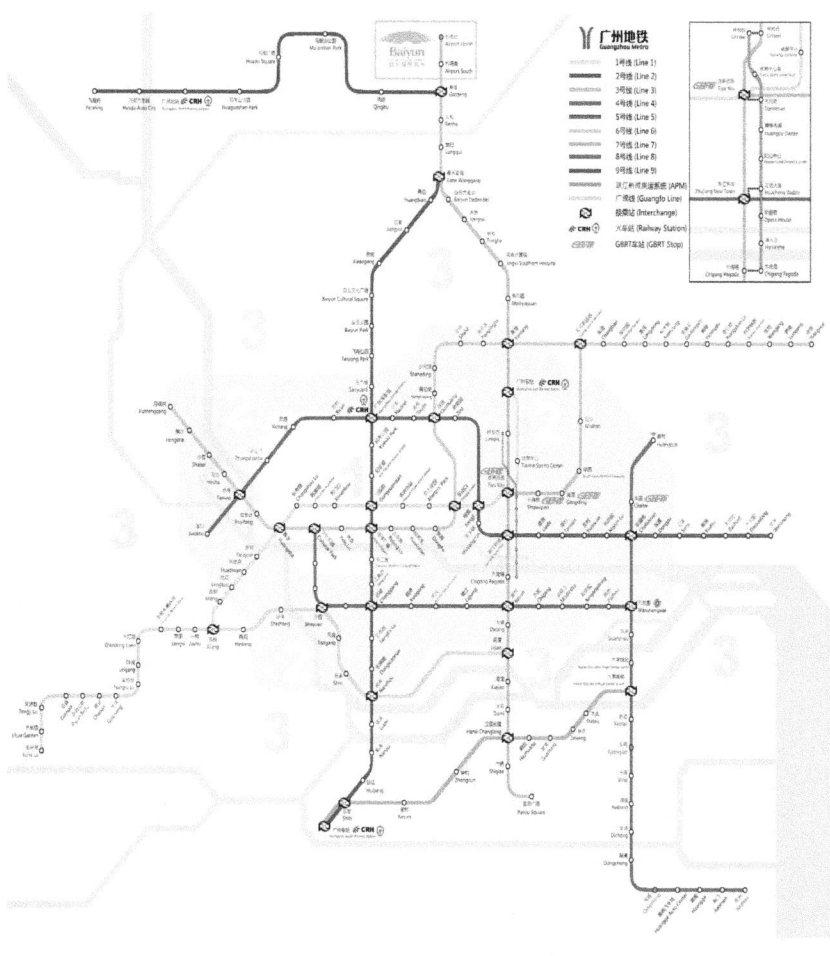

杭州

HANGZHOU

哈尔滨
HARBIN

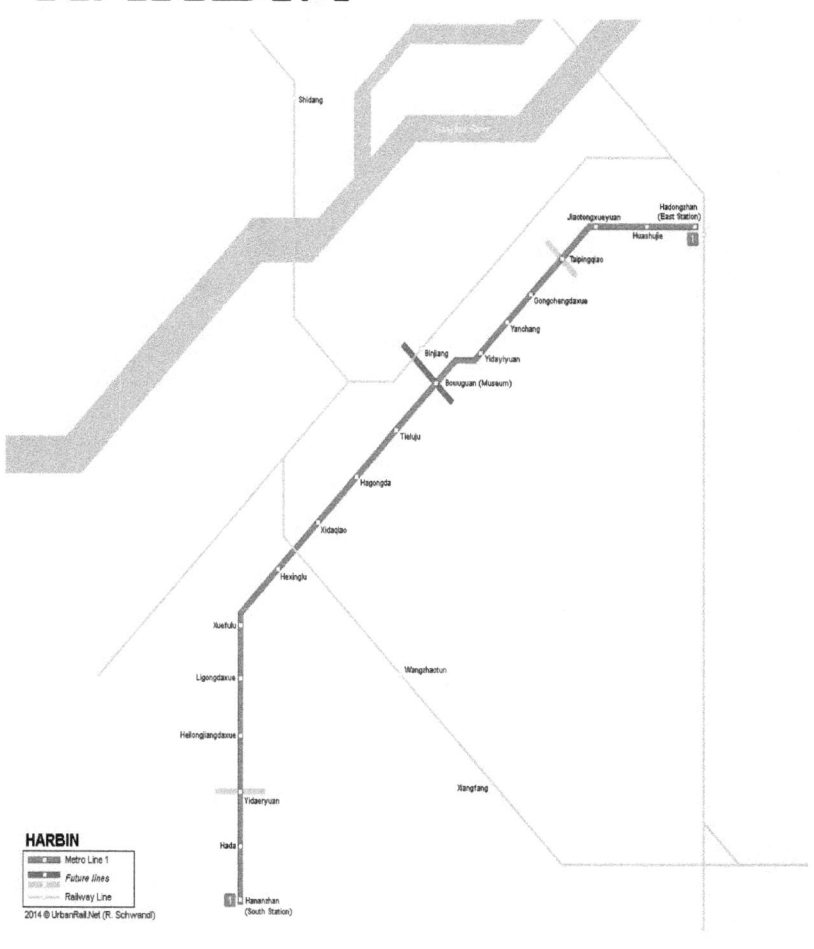

香港
HONG KONG

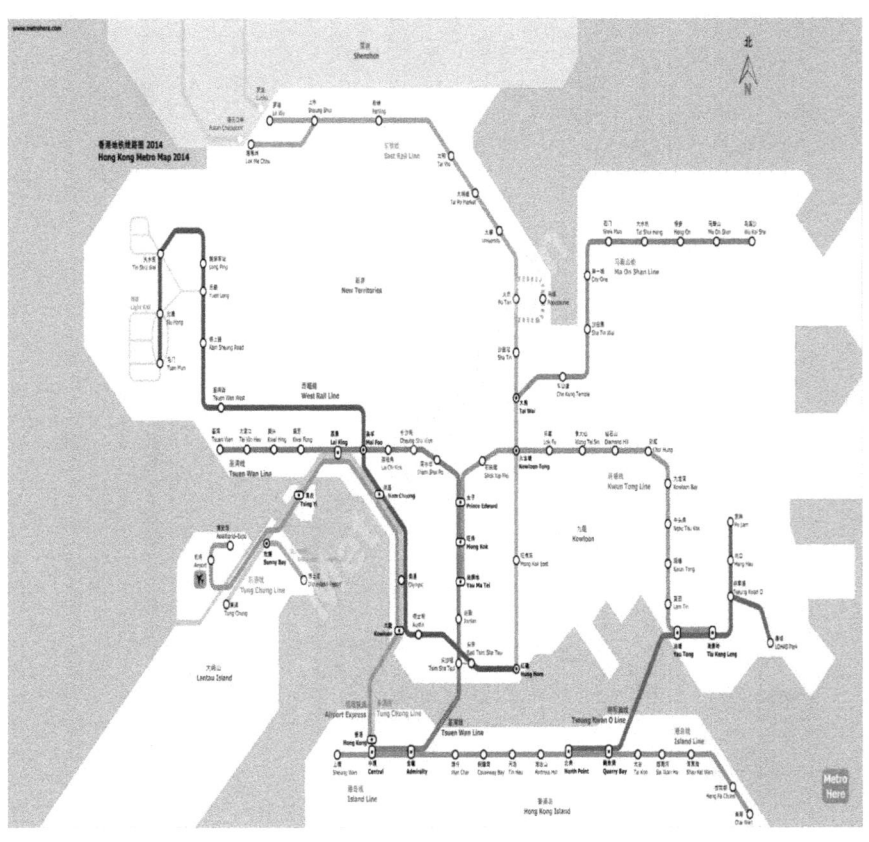

高雄县

KAOHSIUNG

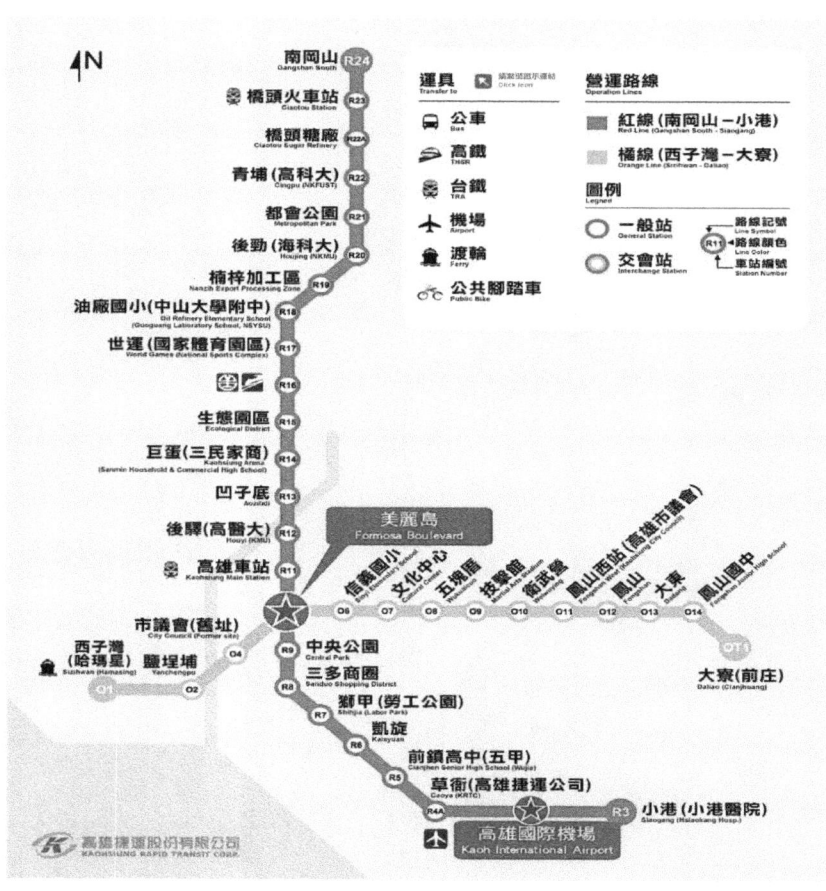

KUNMING

昆明

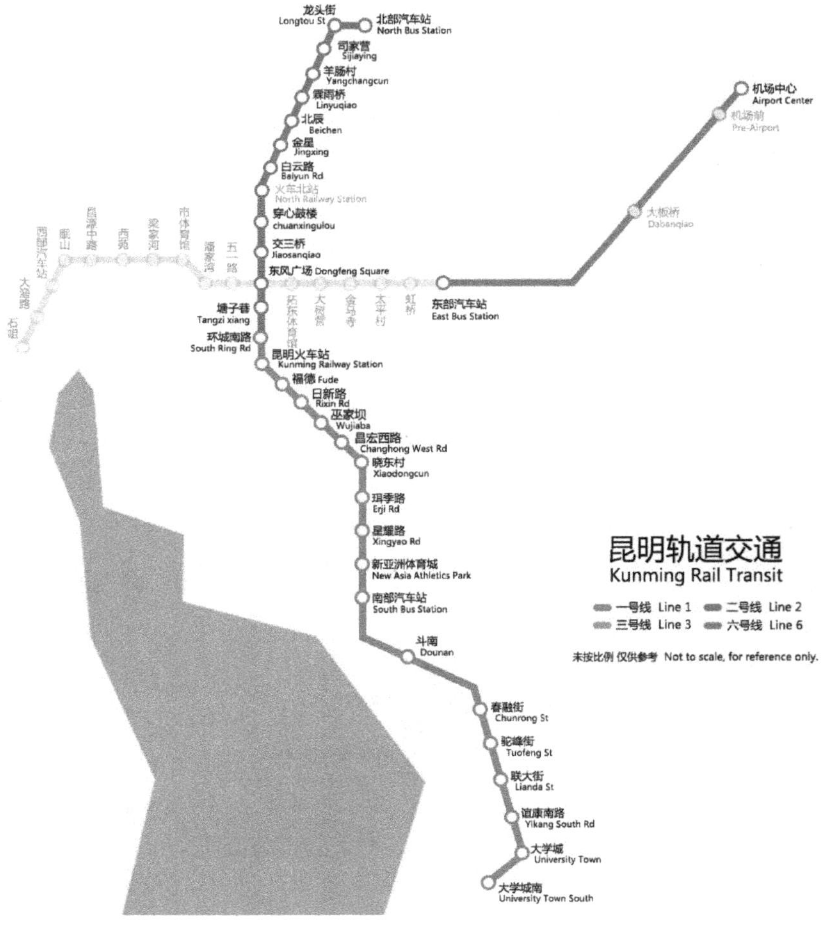
龙头街
Longtou St
北部汽车站
North Bus Station
司家营
Sijiaying
羊肠村
Yangchangcun
霖雨桥
Linyuqiao
北辰
Beichen
金星
Jingxing
白云路
Baiyun Rd
火车北站
North Railway Station
穿心鼓楼
chuanxingulou
交三桥
Jiaosanqiao
东风广场 Dongfeng Square
塘子巷
Tangzi xiang
环城南路
South Ring Rd
昆明火车站
Kunming Railway Station
福德 Fude
日新路
Rixin Rd
巫家坝
Wujiaba
昌宏西路
Changhong West Rd
晓东村
Xiaodongcun
珥季路
Erji Rd
星耀路
Xingyao Rd
新亚洲体育城
New Asia Athletics Park
南部汽车站
South Bus Station
斗南
Dounan
春融街
Chunrong St
驼峰街
Tuofeng St
联大街
Lianda St
宜康南路
Yikang South Rd
大学城
University Town
大学城南
University Town South
西部汽车站
西苑
梁家河
市体育馆
潘家湾
五一路
拓东体育馆
大树营
金马寺
太平村
虹桥
东部汽车站
East Bus Station
大板桥
Dabanqiao
机场前
Pre-Airport
机场中心
Airport Center
昆明轨道交通
Kunming Rail Transit
一号线 Line 1
二号线 Line 2
三号线 Line 3
六号线 Line 6
未按比例 仅供参考 Not to scale, for reference only.

NANJING 南京

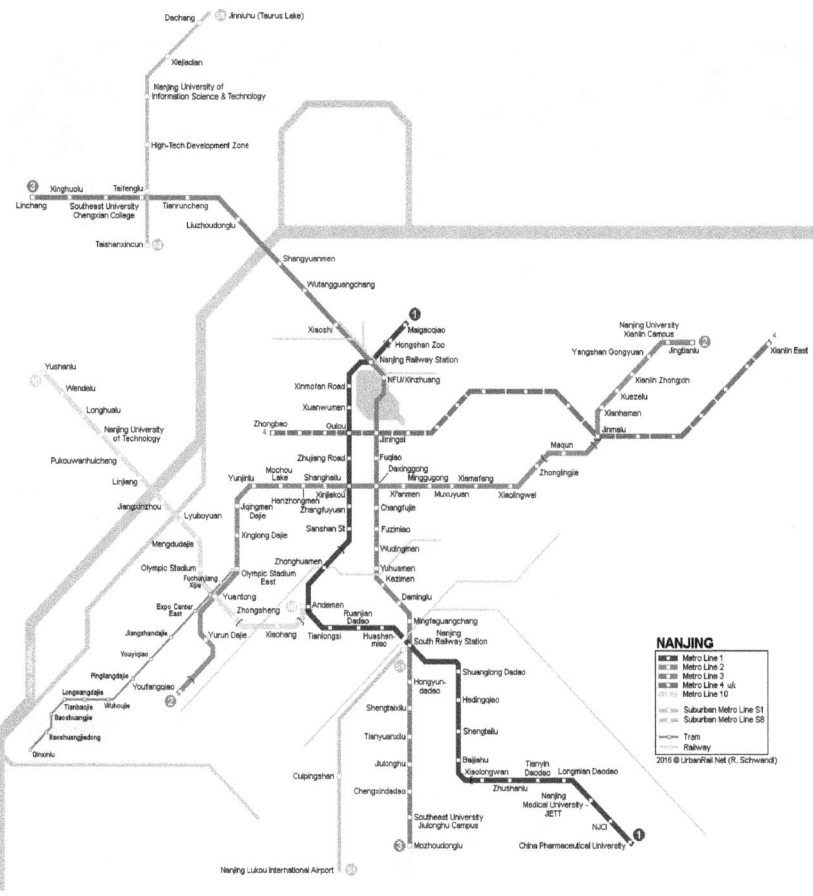

宁波
NINGBO

SHANGHAI

Shanghai Subway Map

1. Xinzhuang - Fujin Rd.
2. Xujing Dong - Pudong Airport
3. Shanghai South Railway Station - Jiangyang North Road
4. Circle
5. Xinzhuang - Minhang Development Area
6. Gangcheng Rd. - Lingyan South Rd.
7. Huamu Rd. - Shanghai University
8. Shiguang Rd. - Aerospace Museum
9. Songjiang New Town - Yanggao Central Rd.
10. Hangzhong Rd. - Xinjiangwan Town
11. Jiangsu Rd. - Anting (Jiading North Rd.)
13. Expo Line (Madang Rd. - Expo Avenue)

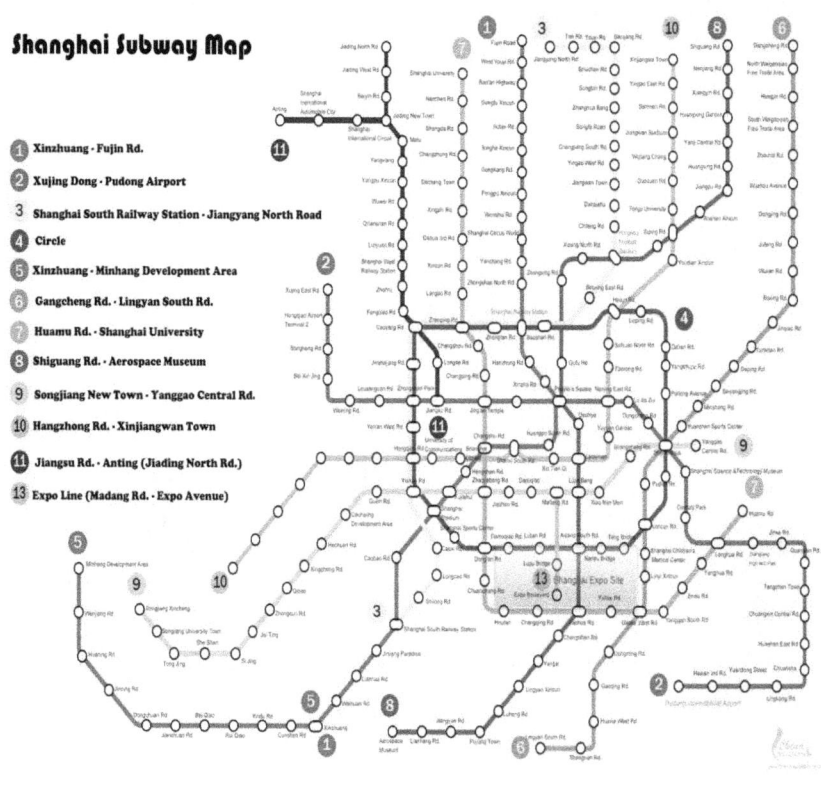

深圳
SHENZHEN

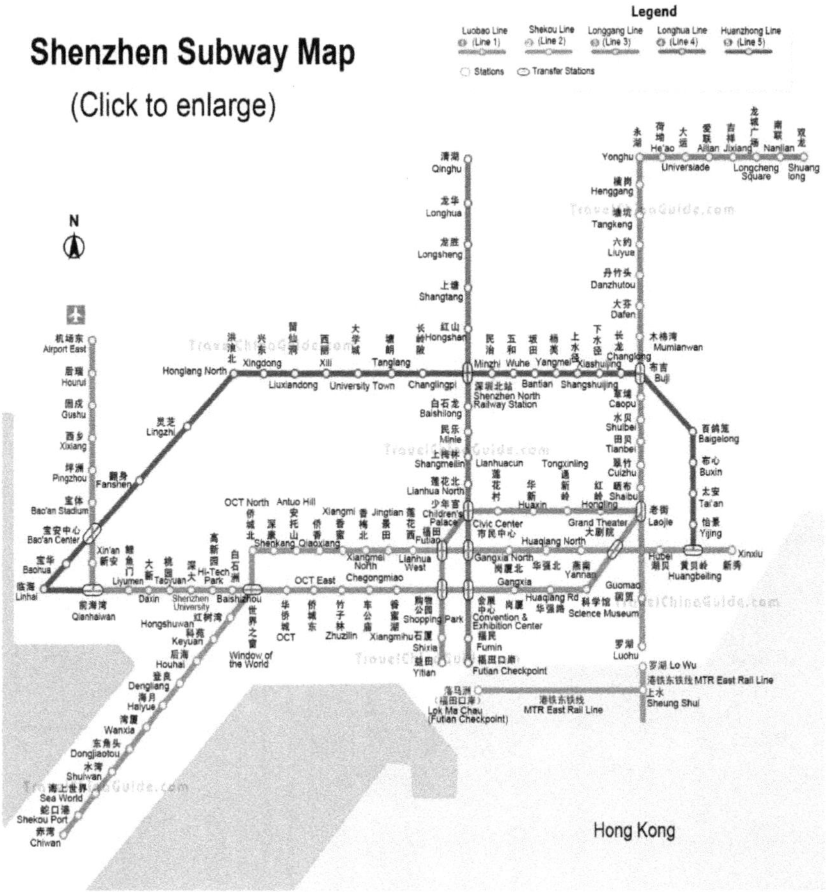
Shenzhen Subway Map
(Click to enlarge)
Legend
Luobao Line (Line 1)
Shekou Line (Line 2)
Longgang Line (Line 3)
Longhua Line (Line 4)
Huanzhong Line (Line 5)
Stations
Transfer Stations
N
Airport East
Hourui
Gushu
Xixiang
Pingzhou
Bao'an Stadium
Bao'an Center
Baohua
Linhai
Qianhaiwan
Fanshen
Lingzhi
Honglang North
Xingdong
Liuxiandong
Xili
University Town
Tanglang
Changlingpi
Hongshan
Qinghu
Longhua
Longsheng
Shangtang
Minzhi
Wuhe
Bantian
Yangmei
Shangshuijing
Xiashuijing
Changlong
Buji
Mumianwan
Shenzhen North Railway Station
Baishilong
Minle
Shangmeilin
Lianhuacun
Tongxinling
Lianhua North
Huaxin
Hongling
Children's Palace
Civic Center
Grand Theater
Laojie
Huaqiang North
Futian
Gangxia North
Yannan
Hubei
Huangbeiling
Xinxiu
Gangxia
Huaqiang Rd
Science Museum
Guomao
Convention & Exhibition Center
Fumin
Futian Checkpoint
Luohu
Lo Wu
MTR East Rail Line
Sheung Shui
Lok Ma Chau (Futian Checkpoint)
Shopping Park
Xiangmihu
Shixia
Yitian
Yonghu
He'ao
Universiade
Ailian
Jixiang
Longcheng Square
Nanlian
Shuanglong
Henggang
Tangkeng
Liuyue
Danzhutou
Dafen
Caopu
Shuibei
Tianbei
Cuizhu
Shaibu
Baigelong
Buxin
Tai'an
Yijing
OCT North
Antuo Hill
Xiangmi
Jingtian
Shenkang
Qiaoxiang
Xiangmei North
Lianhua West
Chegongmiao
OCT East
OCT
Zhuzilin
Window of the World
Baishizhou
Hi-Tech Park
Shenzhen University
Taoyuan
Daxin
Liyumen
Xin'an
Hongshuwan
Keyuan
Houhai
Dengliang
Haiyue
Wanxia
Dongjiaotou
Shuiwan
Sea World
Shekou Port
Chiwan
Hong Kong

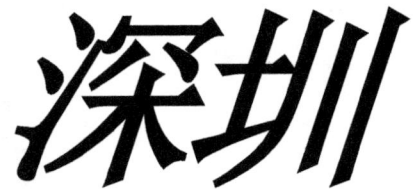

沈阳
SHENYANG

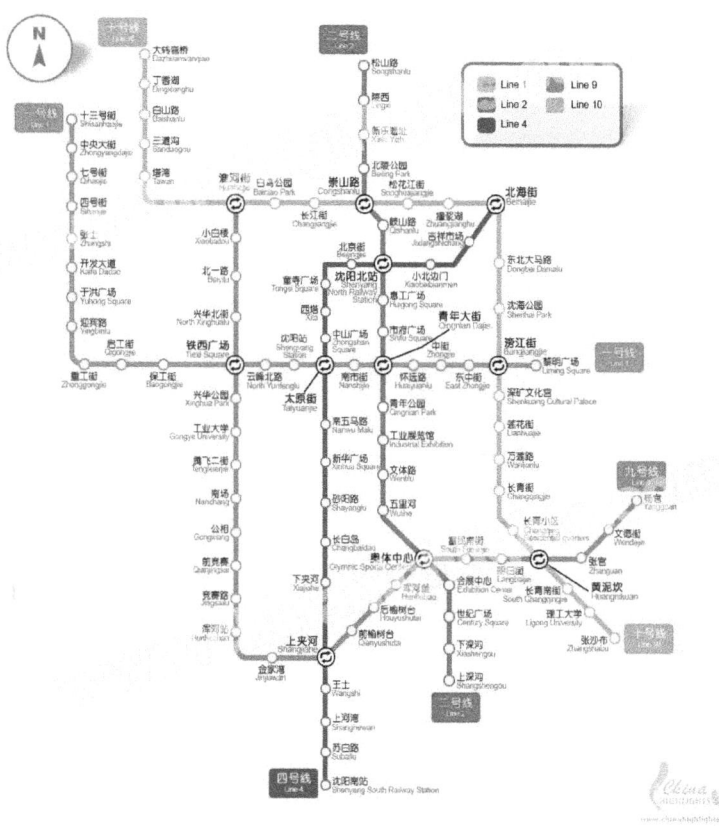

SUZHOU

TAIPEI

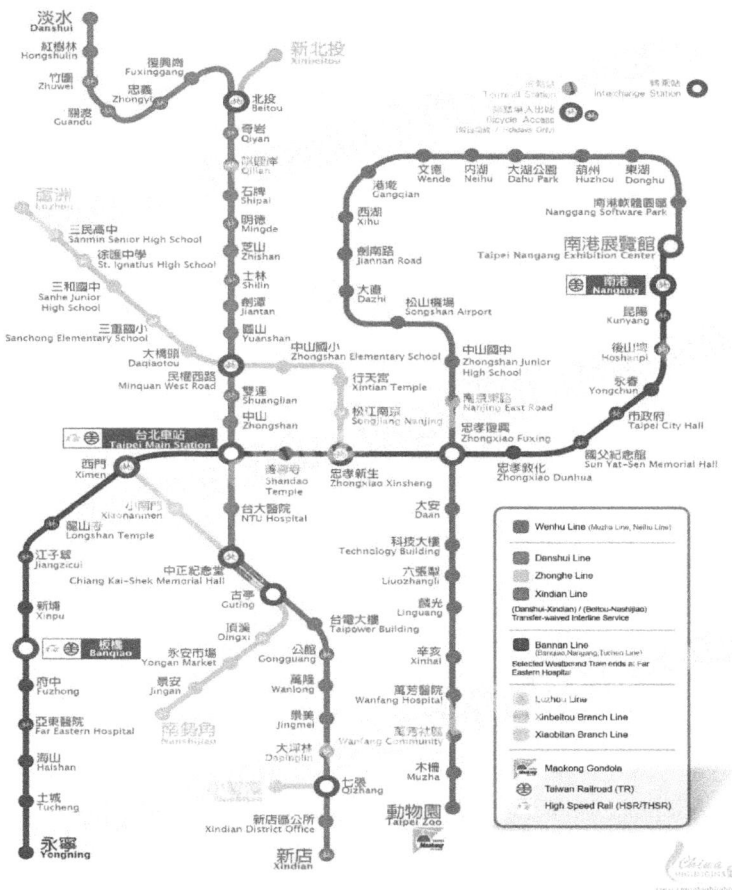

TIANJIN

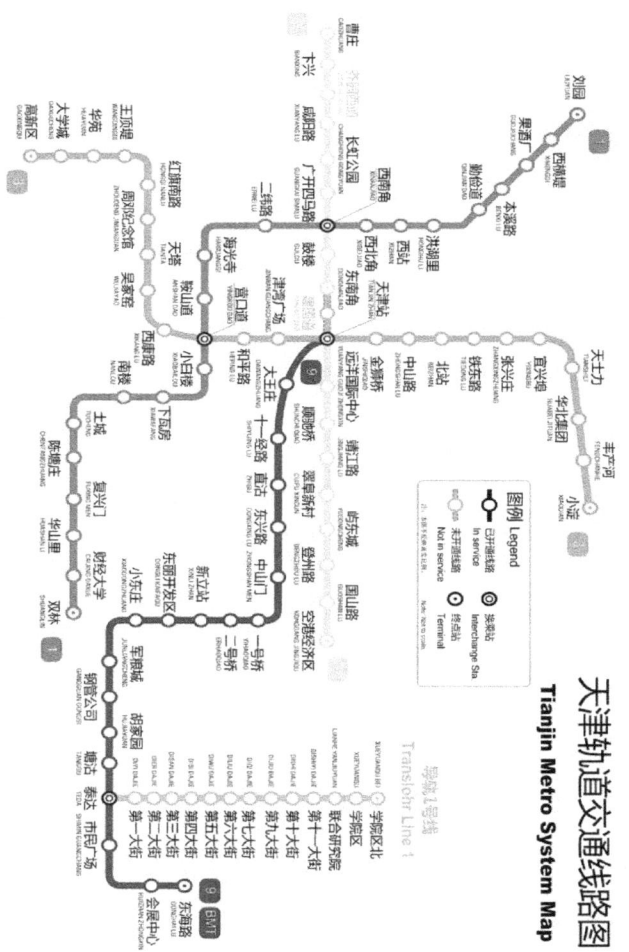

WUHAN
武汉

WUXI

无锡

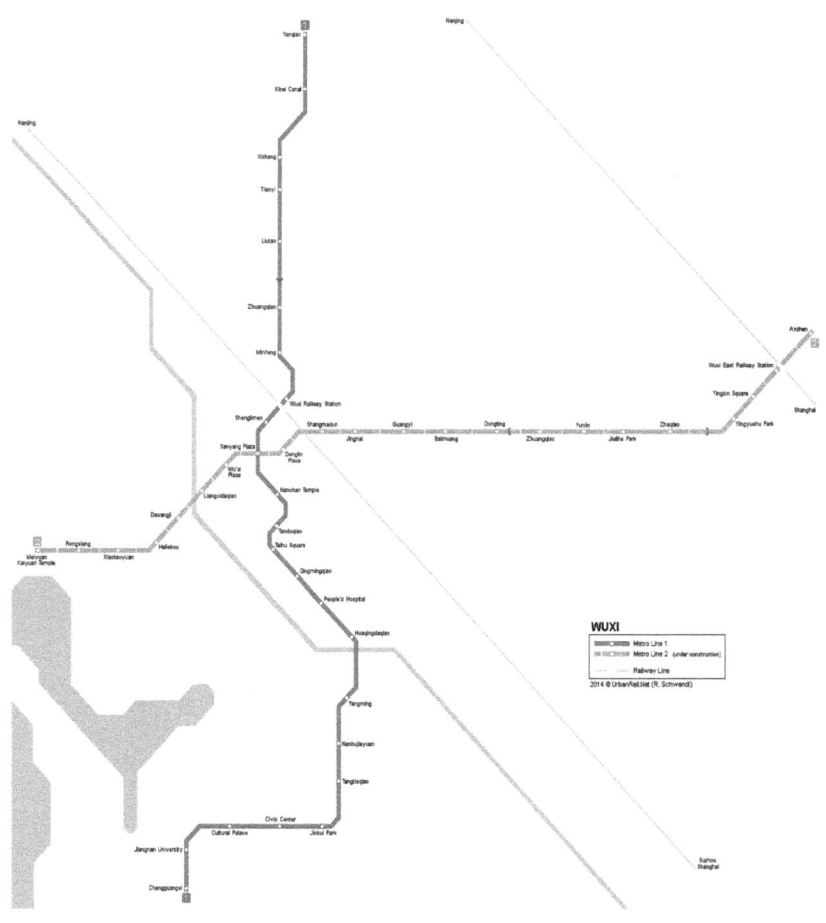

XIAN

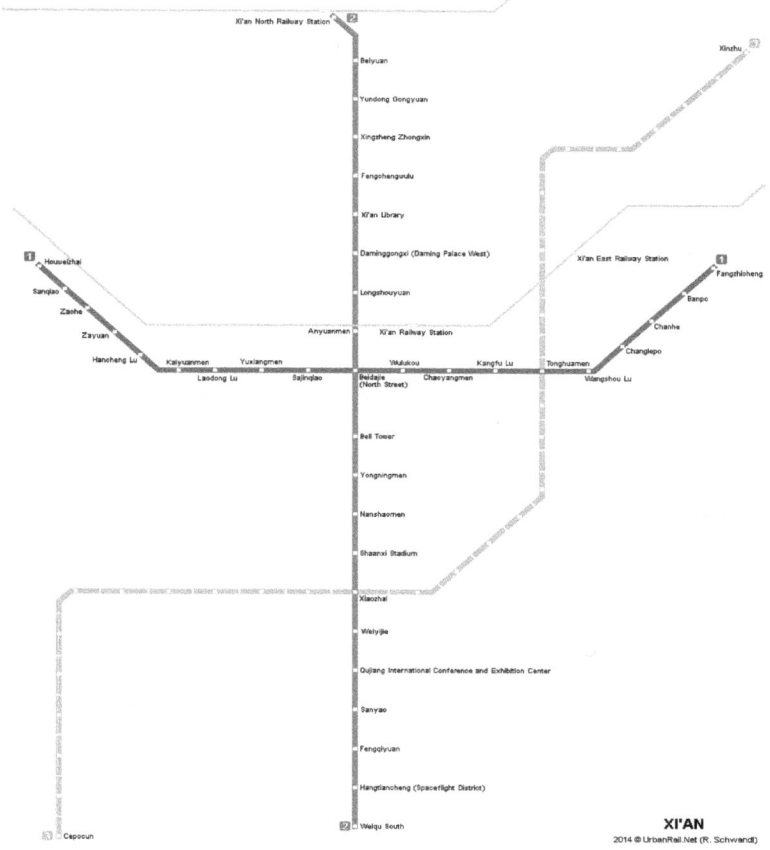

XI'AN
2014 © UrbanRail.Net (R. Schwandl)

ZHENGZHOU
郑州

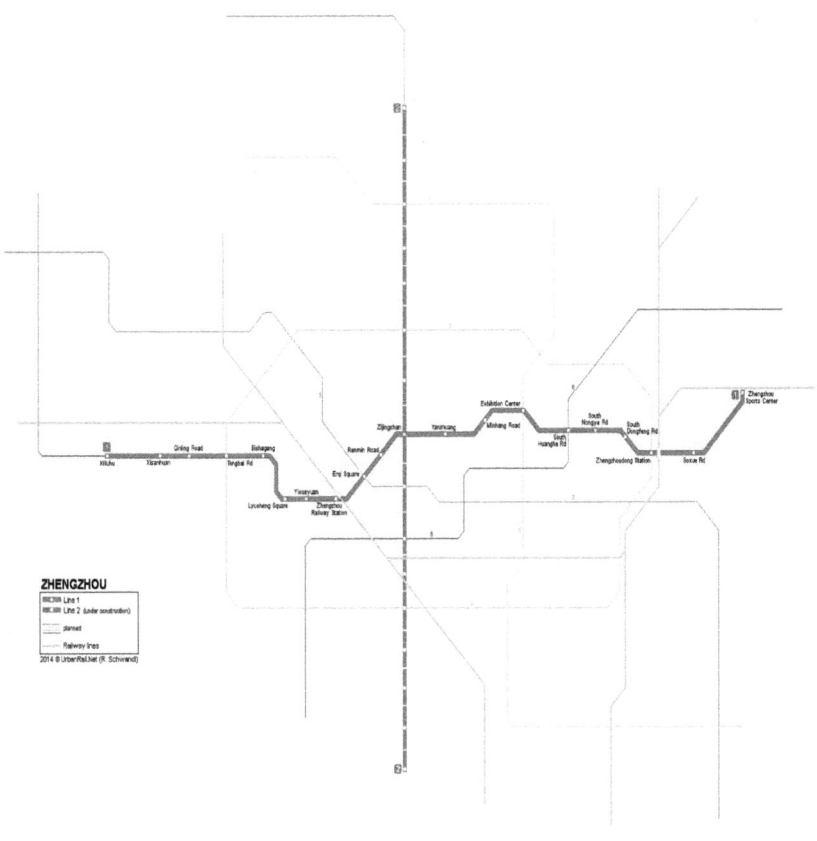

Cultural Transition Stages

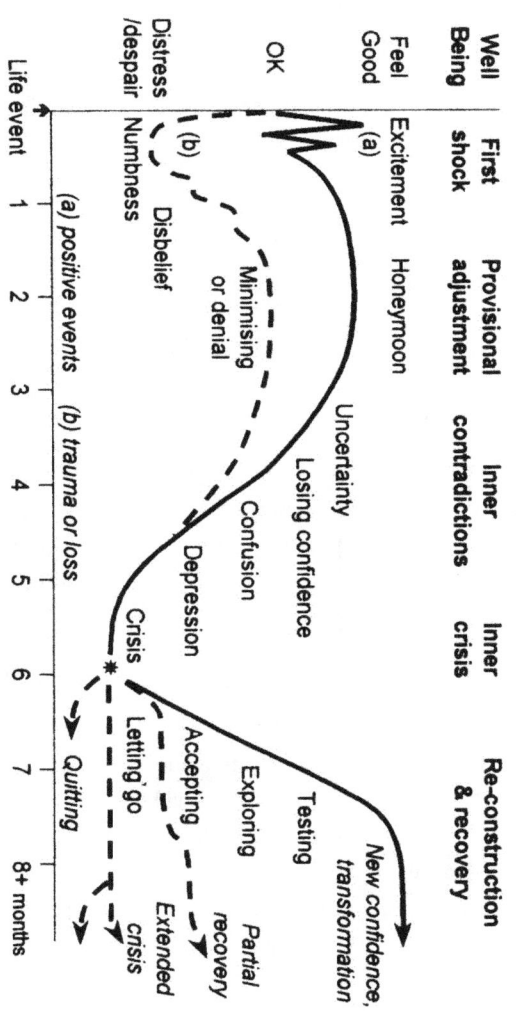

Essential Mandarin

Greetings & Introductions

English	Pinyin	中文
Hello!	Ni hao!	你好！
What's your nationality?	Ni shi na guo ren?	你是哪国人？
I'm American.	Wo shi Meiguoren.	我是美国人。
What's your name?	Ni jiao shenme mingzi?	你叫什么名字？
My name is Julie, and you?	Wo jiao Zhuli, ni ne?	我叫朱丽，你呢？
This is my friend.	Zhe shi wo de pengyou.	这是我的朋友。

Classroom Expressions

English	Pinyin	中文
It is time for class now.	Xianzai shang ke	现在上课。
Let's have a break now.	Xiuxi xiuxi	休息休息。
Class is over.	Xia ke	下课。
Open your textbook, turn to page…	Dakai shu, fan dao di __ ye.	打开书，翻到第__页。
Read after me, please.	Qing gen wo nian.	请跟我念。
Close the book.	He shang shu.	合上书。
Read aloud.	Da dian er sheng.	大点儿声。
Repeat, please.	Qing zai shuo yi bian.	请再说一遍。
Please read.	Qing ni du yi bian.	请你读一遍。
Please answer the question.	Qing ni hui da.	请你回答。
Look at the blackboard.	Qing kan heiban.	请看黑板。
It is correct.	Dui le.	对了。
It is wrong.	Cuo le.	错了。
Very good.	Hen hao.	很好。
Let's do the exercises now.	Xianzai zuo lianxi.	现在做练习。

Ethnic Festivals & Holidays

Ethnic Festivals & Public Holidays 2015/16

Name	中文	Ethnic Group	Details
Losar	洛萨/藏历新年	Tibetan	1st day of Tibetan year; 7 days in Xizang (Tibet)
Sho Dun	雪顿节	Tibetan	30.6 of Tibetan calendar; 7 days in Xizang
Eid ul-Fitr	开斋节/肉孜节	Hui, Uyghur, Kazak, other Muslim groups	1.10 of Islamic calendar; 2 days in Ningxia; 1 day in Xinjiang (Muslims)
Eid al-Adha	古尔邦节	Hui, Uyghur, Kazak, others	End of Ramadan, 10.12 of Islamic calendar; 2 days in Ningxia; 3 days (Muslims) & 1 day for others in Xinjiang
Water-Splashing Festival		Dai	April 14th to 16th
Torch Festival		Yi, Bai, Naxi, etc.	24th to 26th day of the sixth lunar month
Knife-Pole Festival		Lisu	2nd day of the second lunar month
Bullfight Festival		Miao	25th day of the first lunar month
Adult Ceremony		Jino	The day girls turn 15 years old and boys 16 years old
March Fair		Bai, Yi, Hui, Zang (Tibetan), others	15th to 21st day of the third lunar month
Nadam Fair		Mongolian	July or August
Corban Festival		Hui, Uyghur, Kazak, others	The tenth day of the twelfth month on the Islamic calendar

Major TESOL Companies

Company	Website
	EF English First http://www.EF.com
	Wall Street English http://www.wsi.com.cn
	Disney English http://disneyenglish.com
	Shane English http://goldstarteachers.com
	New Oriental http://neworiental.org
	Interlingua School http://interlinguaschool.com
	Berlitz http://berlitz.com
	Meten English http://meteni.com/english

News & Media Resources

Beijing
Beijing Cream | http://beijingcream.com
Beijing Today | http://beijingtoday.com.cn

Chengdu
Go Chengdu | http://gochengdu.com

Kunming
Go Kunming | http://gokunming.com

Hong Kong
South China Morning Post | http://scmp.com

Shanghai
The Shanghaiist | http://shanghaiist.com
Shanghai Daily | http://shanghaidaily.com

Shenzhen
Shenzhen Government | http://english.sz.gov.cn
Shenzhen Daily | http://szdaily.com
Shenzhen Standard | http://shenzhen-standard.com
Shenzhen Party | http://shenzhenparty.org

Countrywide
eChina Cities | http://echinacities.com
China Daily | http://chinadaily.com
SinoShip News | http://sinoshipnews.com
China In Focus | http://chinainfocus.com
Financial Times | http://FT.com
Global Times | http://globaltimes.cn
CCTV News | http://english.cntv.cn

Phonemic Chart
Pronunciation Guide for Learners of English

						iː see	ɪ his	ʊ put	uː too
		p pen	b book	t tea	d day	e ten	ə ago	ɜː her	ɔː saw
		f four	v very	θ thin	ð that	æ hat	ʌ but	ɑː car	ɒ hot
		m man	n no	ŋ sing	h hat				
			l look	s sun	tʃ chair				
			r red	z zoo	dʒ jam	ɪə ear	ʊə pure	eə air	
			w want	ʃ she	k key	eɪ say	ɔɪ boy	aɪ buy	
			j yes	ʒ vision	g go	əʊ so	aʊ now		

CONSONANTS · long sounds · short sounds · DIPTHONGS · voiced consonants · unvoiced consonants

Based on Adrian Underhill's British English Phonemic Chart

Glossary

The following are terms used in the world of TESOL and is of a practical reference. This list is an introduction to TESOL terminology. Chinese cultural terminology is also included.

AAIEP: American Association of Intensive English programs is a group of university and college-based intensive English programs.

Academic language: language used in the learning of academic subject matter in formal schooling context; aspects of language strongly associated with literacy and academic achievement, including specific academic terms or technical language, and speech registers related to each field of study.

Accent: This can mean word stress - control has the accent on the second syllable but we use it to mean the pronunciation used by some speakers - a regional or class accent.

Acculturation: The process of adapting to a new culture. This involves understanding different systems of thought, beliefs, emotions, and communication systems. Acculturation is an important concept for understanding S.L.A., since successful learning is more likely when learners succeed in acculturating.

Accuracy order: Learners learn and produce the L2 with varying degrees of accuracy at different stages of development, perhaps corresponding to the acquisition order.

ACE: Access Certificate in Education. An entry-level training certificate being piloted by Pitmans/City and Guilds in the UK.

ACELS: Advisory Council for English Language Schools in Ireland.

Acquisition: A term used to describe language being absorbed without conscious effort; i.e. the way children pick up their mother tongue. Language acquisition is often contrasted with language learning. The internalization of rules and formulas which are then used to communicate in the L2. For some researchers, such as Krashen, 'acquisition' is unconscious and spontaneous, and 'learning' is conscious, developing through formal study.

Active Vocabulary: The words and phrases which a learner is able to use in speech and writing. Contrasted with Passive Vocabulary.

Advanced: A level of attainment where the learner has mastered most of the structures and functions of the language and is able to move freely through several registers - there may be a working vocabulary of in excess of 3000 words.

Agricultural Bank of China: Also known as ABC or AgBank, is one of the "Big Four" banks in the People's Republic of China. It was founded in 1951 and has headquarters in Dongcheng District, Beijing. http://www.abchina.com/en/default.htm

Aids to Teaching: (a) Visual: Blackboard, whiteboard, overhead projector, realia, posters, wall charts, flipcharts, maps, plans, flashcards, word cards, puppets. (b) Electronic: Tape recorder, TV or video player, computer, CD Rom, language laboratory.

Applied Linguistics: The study of the relationship between theory and practice. The main emphasis is usually on language teaching, but can also be applied to translation, lexicology, among others.

Aptitude: The specific ability a learner has for learning a second language. This is separate from intelligence.

ARELS: Association of Recognized English Language Schools in the UK.

Assessment and Qualifications Alliance (AQA) (formerly AEB & NEAB): Certificate in English Language Skills (ESOL), JET SET, range of graded exams for ESOL.

Assessment standards: Statements that establish guidelines for evaluating student performance and attainment of content standards; often include philosophical statements of good assessment practice (see performance standards).

Attitudes: Learners possess sets of beliefs about language learning, target culture, culture, teacher, learning tasks, etc. These beliefs are referred to as attitudes. They influence learning in a number of ways

Audio-Lingual Method: Listen and speak: this method considers listening and speaking the first tasks in language learning, followed by reading and writing. There is considerable emphasis on learning sentence patterns, memorization of dialogues and extensive use of drills.

Authentic Language: Real or natural language, as used by native speakers of a language in real-life contexts; not artificial or contrived for purposes of learning grammatical forms or vocabulary.

Authentic Task: A task which involves learners in using language in a way that replicates its use in the 'real world' outside the language classroom. Filling in blanks, changing verbs from the simple past to the simple present and completing substitution tables are, therefore, not authentic tasks. Examples of authentic tasks would be answering a letter addressed to the learner, arguing a particular point of view and comparing various holiday brochures in order to decide where to go for a holiday: See pedagogic task.

Authentic Text: A text which is not written or spoken for language teaching purposes. A newspaper article, a rock song, a novel, a radio interview and a traditional fairy tale are examples of authentic texts. A story written to exemplify the use of reported speech, a dialogue scripted to exemplify ways of inviting and a linguistically simplified version of a novel would not be authentic texts: See simplified texts; text.

Auxiliary Verbs: Forms of the verbs be, do and have which are used to create the different tenses in English: am/is/are/was/were eating/ being eaten; do/does/did eat; has/have/had eaten/ been eaten.

Bank of China: Also known as BOC, is one of the five biggest state-owned commercial banks in the People's Republic of China. It was founded in 1912 by the Republican government to replace the Imperial Bank of China. It is the oldest bank in mainland China still in existence. From its establishment until 1942, it issued banknotes on behalf of the government along with the "Big Four" banks. http://www.boc.cn/en/

BASELT: British Association of State English Language Teaching schools in the UK.

BC: British Council.

Behaviorist Learning theory: This a general theory of learning, developed by B F Skinner. It sees learning as the formation of habits. Environmental factors (input, teacher, classroom, etc.) are seen as more important than the student's mental, internal factors.

Biculturalism: Near native like knowledge of two cultures; includes the ability to respond effectively to the different demands of these two cultures.

Bilingual instruction: Provision of instruction in school settings through the medium of two languages, a native and a second language; the proportion of the instructional day delivered in each language varies by the type of the bilingual education program in which instruction is offered and the goals of said program.

Bilingualism: Being able to communicate effectively in two or more languages, with more or less the same degree of proficiency.

Body language: The gestures and mannerisms by which a person communicates with others.

CALL: Computer Assisted Language Learning.

Cambridge: See University of Cambridge.

CAT: Computer Adaptive Testing.

CBT: Computer Based Testing.

CELTA: Certificate in English Language Teaching to Adults. This is a trade name TEFL certificate course developed in the UK by University of Cambridge ESOL (UCLES) and RSA. DELTA is the advanced Diploma course.

CELTYL: Certificate in English Language Teaching to Young Learners. A certificate course developed in the UK by University of Cambridge ESOL (UCLES); normally taken as an add-on option with CELTA.

Cert. TEB: Certificate in Teaching English for Business. A certificate course developed by LCCI for teachers specializing in business English (see LCCI, below).

Cert. TESOL: Certificate in TESOL. The certificate course developed in the UK by Trinity College London. The advanced version for experienced teachers is the Lic. Dip. TESOL.

Cert. TEYL: Certificate in Teaching English to Young Learners. A certificate course extension developed by Trinity College London; normally taken as an add-on option with Cert. TESOL.

Chauncey Group: Part of ETS, US-based group that administers the TOEIC student examination.

China Construction Bank: Also known as CCB, is one of the "Big Four" banks in the People's Republic of China. Founded on October 1, 1954 under the name of People's Construction Bank of China, CCB's name was later changed on March 26, 1996. In 2011, CCB was ranked the second largest bank in the world by market capitalization and the 13th largest company in the world. http://www.ccb.com/en/home/index.html

Chinese Culture: Refers to the customs and traditions of Chinese life and society.

Cloze Procedure: An exercise where every fifth word (or sixth or seventh etc) is deleted from a text. The interval between the deleted words should remain the same throughout the text. The student then supplies the missing words, often relying on contextualization for help.

Cognate: Cognates are words from different languages which are related historically; for example, English bath - German bad or English yoke - Hindi yoga. Beware of False Friends however.

Collocation: The tendency for words to occur regularly with others: sit/chair, house/garage.

Communication Strategies: Strategies for using L2 knowledge. These are used when learners do not have the correct language for the concept they wish to express. Thus they use strategies such as paraphrase and mime: See learner strategies and production strategies.

Communicative Approaches: Approaches to language teaching which aim to help learners to develop communicative competence (i.e., the ability to use the language effectively for communication). A weak communicative approach includes overt teaching of language forms and functions in order to help learners to develop the ability to use them for communication. A strong communicative approach relies on providing learners with experience of using language as the main means of learning to use the language. In such as approach, learners, for example, talk to learn rather than learn to talk.

Communicative Competence: The ability to use the language effectively for communication. Gaining such competence involves acquiring both sociolinguistic and linguistic knowledge (or, in other words, developing the ability to use the language accurately, appropriately, and effectively).

Communicative Functions: Purposes for which language is used; includes three broad functions: communicative, integrative, and expressive; where language aids the transmission of information, aids affiliation and belonging to a particular social group, and allows the display of individual feelings, ideas, and personality.

Communicative Language Teaching: An approach concerned with the needs of students to communicate outside the classroom; teaching techniques reflect this in the choice of language content and materials, with emphasis on role play, pair and group work, among others.

Comprehensible Input: When native speakers and teachers speak to L2 learners, they often adjust their speech to make it more comprehensible. Such comprehensible input may be a necessary condition for acquisition to occur.

Comprehensible Output: The language produced by the learner (the 'output') may be comprehensible or incomprehensible. The efforts learners make to be comprehensible may play a part in acquisition.

Concordances (or concordance lines): A list of authentic utterances each containing the same focused word or phrase e.g.: "The bus driver still didn't have any change so he made me wait. I really don't mind which one. Any newspaper will do. I just ...know what they are saying. Any teacher will tell you that it's ………": See authentic.

Content Words: Words with a full meaning of their own; nouns, main verbs (ie not auxiliary or modal verbs), adjectives and many adverbs. Contrasted with structure words.

Content-based E.S.L.: A model of language education that integrates language and content instruction in the second language classroom; a second language learning approach where second language teachers use instructional materials, learning tasks, and classroom techniques from academic content areas as the vehicle for developing second language, content, cognitive and study skills.

Context: The 'context' of an utterance can mean: i) 'situational context' - the situation in which the utterance is produced; ii) 'linguistic context' - the linguistic environment (the surrounding language).

Contextualization: Placing the target language in a realistic setting, so as to be meaningful to the student.

Contract: An agreement between two or more parties for the doing or not doing of something specific.

Contrastive Analysis Hypothesis: According to this hypothesis, L2 errors are the result of differences between the learner's first language and the target language, and these differences can be used to identify or predict errors that will occur.

Cooperative/Collaborative Group: A grouping arrangement in which positive interdependence and shared responsibility for task completion are established among group members; the type of organizational structure encouraging heterogeneous grouping, shared leadership, and social skills development.

COTE: Certificate for Overseas Teachers of English. A certificate-level course developed by University of Cambridge ESOL (UCLES).

Course book: A textbook which provides the core materials for a course. It aims to provide as much as possible in one book and is designed so that it could serve as the only book which the learners necessarily use during a course. Such a book usually focuses on grammar, vocabulary, pronunciation, functions and the skills of reading, writing, listening and speaking: See supplementary materials.

CRELS: Combined Registered English Language Schools of New Zealand Cross-Cultural.

Competence: Ability to function according to the cultural rules of more than one cultural system; ability to respond in culturally sensitive and appropriate ways according to the cultural demands of a given situation.

Cue Cards: Cards with words or pictures on them which are used to encourage student response, or pair and group work.

Culture: The sum total of the ways of life of a people; includes norms, learned behavior patterns, attitudes, and artifacts; also involves traditions, habits or customs; how people behave, feel and interact; the means by which they order and interpret the world; ways of perceiving, relating and interpreting events based on established social norms; a system of standards for perceiving, believing, evaluating, and acting.

DELTA: Diploma in English Language Teaching to Adults. The advanced (post-experience) qualification from University of Cambridge ESOL (UCLES).

Dialect: The regional variety of a language, differing from the standard language, in grammar, vocabulary, pronunciation or idiomatic usage.

Direct Method: The most common approach in TEFL, where language is taught through listening and speaking. There may be little or no explicit explanation dealing with syntax or grammatical rules, nor translation into the mother tongue of the student - inductive learning rather than deductive.

Discourse: Unit of language greater than a sentence: language in action or performance communicatively.

DOS: Director of Studies Drilling: The intensive and repetitive practice of the target language, which may be choral or individual.

Dynasty: A sequence of rulers from the same family, stock, or group. For example, *"the Song Dynasty."*

E.F.L.: English as a foreign language.
E.S.L.: L2: English as a Second Language. The field of English as a second language; courses, classes and/or programs designed for students learning English as an additional language.

E.S.O.L.: student: English to speakers of other languages; refers to learners who are identified as still in the process of acquiring English as an additional language; students who may not speak English at all or, at least, do not speak, understand, and write English with the same facility as their classmates because they did not grow up speaking English (rather they primarily spoke another language at home).

E.S.O.L.: English to / for Speakers of Other Languages.

E.S.P.: English for Specific Purposes; e.g., for business, science and technology, medicine among others.

EAP: English for Academic Purposes – The study or teaching of English with specific reference to an academic (usually a university - or college-based) course.

ECIS: European Council of International Schools.

EFL: English as a Foreign Language – English language programs in countries where English is not the common or official language. It is used in American university programs where international students study English although the use of the word "foreign" is now avoided in some schools because of its xenophobic connotations.

Elementary: Students at this level may have a vocabulary of up to 1000 words and will probably be learning or practicing present simple and continuous tenses, past simple and present perfect, will/shall, 'going to' futures. They should be able to hold simple conversations and survive in everyday situations.

ELICOS: English Language Intensive Courses for Overseas Students. The Australian term for EFL.

ELL: English Language Learner–a term that has become popular in California designed to replace the acronym "LEP" (see below) which many teachers felt to be pejorative.

ELT: English Language Teaching or Training–A term coined in the UK and designed to replace EFL. It is in use around the world but has yet to catch on in the USA.

ELTAs: English Language Teacher Associations groups for teachers in Germany and Austria.

English: The English language, composition, and literature as offered as a course of study.

EOP: English for Occupational Purposes.

Error Analysis: In this procedure, samples of learner language are collected and the errors are identified, described, and classified according to their hypothesized causes. The errors are then evaluated for relative seriousness.

ESB: English Speaking Board International. Oral assessments in (spoken) English

ESL: English as a Second Language – English language programs in countries where English is the dominant or official language. Programs designed for non-English-speaking immigrants in the USA are ESL programs.

ESOL: English to Speakers of Other Languages–a term often used to describe elementary and secondary English language programs. It is sometimes used to distinguish ESL classes within adult basic education programs.

ESP: English for Specific Purposes–a term that refers to teaching or studying English for a particular career (like law or medicine) or for business in general.

ETS: (Educational Testing Service) Based in Princeton, NJ, the world's biggest examination board, administrators of the TOEFL student examination.

Experiential: Referring to ways of learning language through experiencing in use rather than through focusing conscious attention on language items. Reading a novel, listening to a song and taking part in a project are experiential ways of learning a language.

Extensive Reading: Reading for general or global understanding, often of longer texts.

False Friends: Cognate words, or words accidentally similar in form, whose meaning is rather different in the two languages, e.g., English gentle - French gentil.

Feedback: The response learners get when they attempt to communicate. This can involve correction, acknowledgement, requests for clarification, backchannel cues (e.g., "mmm"). Feedback plays an important role in helping learners to test their ideas about the target language.

Filter: Learners do not attend to all the input they receive. They attend to some features, and 'filter' other features out. This often depends on affective factors such as motivation, attitudes, emotions, and anxiety.

First Certificate: Cambridge First Certificate: an examination which may be taken by students of a good intermediate level.

Foreign language: A language which is not normally used for communication in a particular society. Thus English is a foreign language in France and Spanish is a foreign language in Germany.

Formal instruction: This occurs in classrooms when teachers try to aid learning by raising the learners' consciousness about the target language rules. Formal instruction can be deductive (the learners are told the rules) or inductive (learners develop a knowledge of the rules through carrying out language tasks).

Frequency: The input language contains a range of linguistic forms which occur with varying frequency. The learner's output also contains a range of linguistic forms used with varying frequency. There is evidence to show that input frequency matches output frequency. Function Words: See Structure Words.

Functions: the things people do through language, for example, instructing, apologizing, complaining. Functional Approach: A course based on a functional approach would take as its starting point for language development, what the learner wants to do through language. Common functions include identifying oneself and giving personal facts about oneself; expressing moods and emotions.

Genre: A category of literary composition characterized by a particular style, form, or content (e.g., an historical novel is one fictional genre).

Global course book: A course book which is not written for learners from a particular culture or country but which is intended for use by any class of learners in the specified level anywhere in the world.

Grading: The order in which language items are taught. Systematic grading may reduce the difficulties of language learning by introducing the language in steps or stages.

Grammar-Translation: A method based upon memorizing the rules and logic of a language and the practice of translation. Traditionally the means by which Latin and Greek have been taught.

Grapheme: The written symbols for sounds in language; i.e., letters of the alphabet or a character in picture writing (as in Japanese kange).

Home language: Language(s) spoken in the home by significant others (e.g., family members, caregivers) who reside in the child's home; sometimes used as a synonym for first language, primary language, or native language.

Hypothesis formation: According to this concept, the learner forms hypotheses about the target-language rules, and then tests them out. These are internalized rules, which are used in L2 communication.

IATEFL: International Association of Teachers of English as a Foreign Language is based in the UK with members around the world.

Idiolect: The individual's language in a given tongue or code (e.g., 'English' for a given American user; 'Spanish' for a Mexican one).

Idiom: An expression in the usage of a language that has a meaning that cannot be derived from the conjoined meanings of its elements (e.g., raining cats and dogs).

IEP: Intensive English Program—refers to an intensive course designed to help non-English speaking students prepare for academic study at a university or college.

Immersion Method: This simulates the way in which children acquire their mother tongue. The learner is surrounded by the foreign language, with no deliberate or organized teaching program. The learner absorbs the target language naturally without conscious effort.

Inductive Learning: Learning to apply the rules of a language by experiencing the language in use, rather than by having the rules explained or by consciously deducing the rules.

Industrial and Commercial Bank of China: Also known as ICBC, is the largest bank in the world by total assets. Founded as a limited company on January 1, 1984, it is one of China's "Big Four" state-owned commercial banks. http://www.icbc.com.cn/ICBC/sy/default.htm

Inferencing: This is the means by which the learner forms hypotheses, through attending to input, or using the situational context to interpret the input.

Inflection: The change in form of a word, which indicates a grammatical change. For example: behave - behaved - behavior - misbehave.

Input: This constitutes the language to which the learner is exposed. It can be spoken or written. It serves as the data which the learner must use to determine the rules of the target language.

Intensive Reading: Reading for specific understanding of information, usually of shorter texts.

Interactional tasks: Tasks which promote communication and interaction. The idea behind this approach is that the primary purpose of speech is the maintenance of social relationships: See transactional tasks.

Interference: According to behaviorist learning theory, the patterns of the learner's mother tongue (L1) get in the way of learning the patterns of the L2. This is referred to as 'interference'.

Interlanguage: The learner's knowledge of the L2 which is independent of both the L1 and the actual L2. This term can refer to: i) the series of interlocking systems which characterize acquisition; ii) the system that is observed at a single stage of development (an 'interlanguage'); and iii) particular L1/L2 combinations.

Intermediate: At this level a student will have a working vocabulary of between 1500 and 2000 words and should be able to cope easily in most everyday situations. There should be an ability to express needs, thoughts and feelings in a reasonably clear way.

IELTS: International English Language Testing System. Managed by UCLES, the British Council and IDP Australia for academic and vocational English.

Intonation: The ways in which the voice pitch rises and falls in speech.

L.A.D.: Language Acquisition Device; a term coined by Noam Chomsky to explain an innate psychological capacity for language acquisition.

L1: First language

L1: The mother tongue.

L2: A term used to refer to both foreign and second languages: See foreign language; second language.

L2: Second language.

Language "chunks": Short phrases learned as a unit (e.g., thank you very much); patterned language acquired through redundant use, such as refrains and repetitive phrases in stories.

Language awareness: Approaches to teaching language which emphasize the value of helping learners to focus attention on features of language in use. Most such approaches emphasize the importance of learners gradually developing their own awareness of how the language is used through discoveries which they make themselves: See discovery activities.

Language data: Instances of language use which are used to provide information about how the language is used. Thus a corpus can be said to consist of language data: See corpus.

Language Laboratory: A room equipped with headphones and booths to enable students to listen to a language teaching program, while being monitored from a central console. Labs may be Audio-Active (AA), where students listen and respond to a tape, or Audio-Active-Comparative (AAC), where they may record their own responses and compare these with a model on the master tape.

Language practice: Activities which involve repetition of the same language point or skill in an environment which is controlled by the framework of the activity. The purpose for language production and the language to be produced are usually predetermined by the task of the teacher. The intention is not to use the language for communication but to strengthen, through successful repetition, the ability to manipulate a particular language form or function. Thus getting all the students in a class who already know each other repeatedly to ask each other their names would be a practice activity: See language use.

Language proficiency: The level of competence at which an individual is able to use language for both basic communicative tasks and academic purposes.

Language use: Activities which involve the production of language in order to communicate. The purpose of the activity might be predetermined but the language which is used is determined by the learners. Thus, getting a new class of learners to walk round and introduce themselves to each other would be a language use activity, and so would be getting them to complete a story.

Language variety: Variations of a language used by particular groups of people, includes regional dialects characterized by distinct vocabularies, speech patterns, grammatical features, and so forth; may also vary by social group (sociolect) or idiosyncratically for a particular individual (idiolect).

Learning strategies: These account for how learners accumulate new L2 rules and how they automate existing ones. They can be conscious or subconscious. These contrast with communication strategies and production strategies, which account for how the learners use their rule systems, rather than how they acquire them. Learning strategies may include metacognitive strategies (e.g., planning for learning, monitoring one's own comprehension and production, evaluating one's performance); cognitive strategies (e.g., mental or physical manipulation of the material), or social/affective strategies (e.g., interacting with another person to assist learning, using self-talk to persist at a difficult task until resolution).

Learning styles: The way(s) that particular learners prefer to learn a language. Some have a preference for hearing the language (auditory learners), some for seeing it written down (visual learners), some for learning it in discrete bits (analytic learners), some for experiencing it in large chunks (global or holistic or experiential learners) and many prefer to do something physical whilst experiencing the language (kinesthetic learners).

Learning: The internalization of rules and formulas which can be used to communicate in the L2. Krashen uses this term for formal learning in the classroom.

LEP: Limited English Proficient—a term used for many years to designate children in the schools systems for whom English was not their first language. Now replaced by terms like ELL.

Lexical item: An item of vocabulary which has a single element of meaning. It may be a compound or phrase: bookcase, post office, put up with. Some single words may initiate several lexical items; eg letter: a letter of the alphabet / posting a letter.

Lexical set: A group or family of words related to one another by some semantic principle: eg lamb, pork, chicken, beef are all different types of meat and form a lexical set.

Linguistic Competence: A broad term used to describe the totality of a given individual's language ability; the underlying language system believed to exist as inferred from an individual's language performance.

LCCIEB: London Chamber of Commerce and Industry. Range of business and specialist English examinations.

London Examinations: Edexcel International London Tests of English range of exams graded from basic to proficient.

LTCL. Dip. TESOL: Licentiate Diploma in TESOL. The advanced (post-experience) qualification from Trinity College London.

Materials adaptation: Making changes to materials in order to improve them or to make them more suitable for a particular type of learner. Adaptation can include reducing, adding, omitting, modifying and supplementing. Most teachers adapt materials every time they use a textbook in order to maximize the value of the book for their particular learners.

Materials evaluation: The systematic appraisal of the value of materials in relation to their objectives and to the objectives of the learners using them. Evaluation can be pre-use and therefore focused on predictions of potential value. It can be whilst-use and therefore focused on awareness and description of what the learners are actually doing whilst the materials are being used. And it can also be post-use and therefore focused on analysis of what happened as a result of using the materials.

Materials: Anything which is used to help to teach language learners. Materials can be in the form of a textbook, a workbook, a cassette, a CD-Rom, a video, a photocopied handout, a newspaper, a paragraph written on a whiteboard: anything which presents of informs about the language being learned.

Meaning-focused tasks: These tasks focus on communication of meaning. Meaning-focused tasks do not provide practice activities which focus on individual linguistic components as a preliminary to engagement in communicative tasks. According to the meaning-focused approach, involvement in communicative tasks is all that is necessary to develop competence in a second language: See form-focused tasks.

Micro-teaching: A technique used on teacher training courses: a part of a lesson is taught to a small number of students. A variation of this is 'peer teaching', where the 'students' are often peers of the trainee teacher attending the same course.

Minimal Pair: A pair of items differing by one phonological feature; for example: sit/set, ship/sheep, pen/pan, fan/pan, pan/pat, among others.

Ministry of Education of the People's Republic of China: An agency of the State Council which regulates all aspects of the educational system in mainland China. This includes compulsory basic education, vocational education, and tertiary education. The Ministry certifies teachers, standardizes curriculum and textbooks, establishes standards and generally monitors the entire education system in an effort to modernize China through education.

Modal Verb: Verbs which express the mood of another verb: will/would; shall/should; may/might; can/could; must, ought, need, dare, used to.

Monitor: Language learners and native speakers typically try to correct any errors in what they have just said. This is referred to as 'monitoring'. The learner can monitor vocabulary, phonology, or discourse. Krashen uses 'Monitoring' to refer the way the learner uses 'learnt' knowledge to improve naturally 'acquired' knowledge.

Morpheme: The smallest unit of language that is grammatically significant. Morphemes may be bound; that is, they cannot exist on their own. For example, er, un, ed, mis, among others. Or, they can be free, as is ball in football, a compound noun comprised of such word plus 'foot'.

Morphology: The branch of linguistics which studies how words change their forms when they change grammatical function, i.e., their inflections swim - swam - swum - swimming - swimmer; cat - cats; mouse - mice; happy - happier – happily, among others: See also Syntax.

Motivation: This can be defined in terms of the learner's overall goal or orientation. 'Instrumental' motivation occurs when the learner's goal is functional (e.g. to get a job or pass an examination), and 'integrative' motivation occurs when the learner wishes to identify with the culture of the L2 group. "Task" motivation is the interest felt by the learner in performing different learning tasks.

Multilingualism: Ability to speak more than two languages; proficiency in many languages.

Multi-media materials: Materials which make use of a number of different media. Often they are available on a CD-Rom which makes use of print, graphics, video and sound. Usually such materials are interactive and enable the learner to receive feedback on the written or spoken language which they produce.

Multiple intelligences. (Also MI): A theory of intelligence that characterizes human intelligence as having multiple dimensions that must be acknowledged and developed in education. The theory of MI is based on the work of the psychologist Gardner who posits 8 intelligences.

NABE: National Association for Bilingual Education is an association that represents the interests of bilingual teachers in the USA.

Native language: Primary or first language spoken by an individual: (See L1).

Natural Approach: Pioneered by Krashen, this approach combines acquisition and learning as a means of facilitating language development in adults.

NEAS: National ELT Accreditation Scheme, for course-providers in Australia.

Neuro-linguistic Programming. (Also NLP): A training philosophy and set of training techniques first developed by John Grindler and Richard Bandler in the mid -1970s as an alternative form of therapy. Important within language teaching to teachers interested in humanistic approaches, i.e. those which focus on developing one's sense of self-actualization and self-awareness.

Nonverbal Communication: Paralinguistic and non linguistic messages that can be transmitted in conjunction with language or without the aid of language; paralinguistic mechanisms include intonation, stress, rate of speech, and pauses or hesitations; non linguistic behaviors include gestures, facial expressions, and body language, among others.

Notions: General concepts expressed through language such as temporality, duration, and quantity. Over-generalization: Language learners often produce errors which are extensions of general rules to items not covered by the rules. For example, 'I comed home' *. This is called 'over-generalization'.

Pair Work: A process in which students work in pairs for practice or discussion. particular career (like law or medicine) or for business in general.

Passive Vocabulary: The vocabulary that students are able to understand compared to that which they are able to use. Contrasted with Active Vocabulary.

Patterns: These are a type of formulaic speech. They are unanalyzed units which have open slots. For example: 'Can I have a ....?': See formulaic speech and routines.

Pedagogic task: In pedagogic tasks, learners are required to do things which it is extremely unlikely they would be called upon to do outside of the classroom. Completing one half of a dialogue, filling in the blanks in a story and working out the meaning of ten nonsense words from clues in a text would be examples of pedagogic tasks: See real-world tasks.

Peer Group: Usually refers to people working or studying at the same level or in the same grouping; one's colleagues or fellow students.

Performance standards: Statements that refer to how well students are meeting a content standard; specify the quality and effect of student performance at various levels of competency (benchmarks) in the subject matter; specify how students must demonstrate their knowledge and skills and can show student progress toward meeting a standard.

Phoneme: The smallest unit of sound which causes a change of meaning: cattle - kettle /kæte/.

Pitman Qualifications: Range of general ESOL exams, including spoken English and business English.

Process approach: The process approach focuses on the means whereby learning occurs. The process is more important than the product. In terms of writing, the important aspect is the way in which completed text was created. The act of composing evolves through several stages as writers discover, through the process, what it is that they are trying to say: See product approach.

Product approach: The product approach focuses on the end result of teaching/learning. In terms of writing, there should be something "resulting" from the composition lesson (e.g. letter, essay, story, etc.). This result should be readable, grammatically correct and obeying discourse conventions relating to main points, supporting details and so on: See process approach.

Production strategies: These refer to utilization of linguistic knowledge in communication. They do not imply any communication problem (cf., communication strategies) and they operate largely unconsciously: See communication strategies and learning strategies.

Rate of acquisition: The speed at which the learner develops L2 proficiency. This is different to the 'route of acquisition'. Register: The kind of language used by particular groups for particular communicative situations, for example law register.

RELSA: Recognized English Language Schools Association. The organization of independent language schools in Ireland RSA Royal Society of Arts is a body that works with UCLES (see below).

S.L.A.: This is an abbreviation for Second Language Acquisition and is normally used to refer to research and theory related to the learning of second and foreign languages.

Schema theory: A theory of language processing based on the notion that past experiences lead to the creation of mental frameworks that help us make sense of new experiences.

Second language: The term is used to refer to a language which is not a mother tongue but which is used for certain communicative functions in a society. Thus English is a second language in Nigeria, Sri Lanka and Singapore. French is a second language in Senegal, Cameroon and Tahiti: See foreign language.

Self-access materials: Materials designed for learners to use independently (i.e., on their own without access to a teacher or a classroom). They are normally used by the learner at home, in a library or in a self-study center.

Simplified texts: These are texts which have been made simpler so as to make it easier for learners to read them. The usual principles of simplification involve reduction in length of the text, shortening of sentences, omission or replacement of difficult words or structures, omission of qualifying clauses and omission of non-essential detail. It is arguable, however, that such simplification might make the words easier to understand

but could make it more difficult for the learners to achieve global understanding of a text which is now dense with important information. It might be more profitable to simplify texts by adding examples, by using repetition and paraphrase and by increasing redundant information. In other words, by lengthening rather than shortening the text.

Supplementary materials: Materials designed to be used in addition to the core materials of a course. They are usually related to the development of skills of reading, writing, listening or speaking rather than to the learning of language items: See course book.

Target language: This is the language that the learner is attempting to learn. It comprises the native speaker's grammar.

Task based: This refers to materials or courses which are designed around a series of authentic tasks which give learners experience of using the language in ways in which it is used in the 'real world' outside the classroom. They have no pre-determined language syllabus and the aim is for learners to learn from the tasks the language they need to participate successfully in them. Examples of such tasks would be working out the itinerary of a journey from a timetable, completing a passport application form, ordering a product from a catalogue and giving directions to the post office: See authentic tasks.

Teacher talk: Teachers make adjustments to both language form and language function in order to help communication in the classroom. These adjustments are called 'teacher talk'.

TEFL: Teaching English as a Foreign Language – a term that refers to teacher training programs in EFL.

TESL: Teaching English as a Second Language, Canada - national federation of teachers and providers in Canada.

TESL: Teaching English as a Second Language – a term that refers to teacher training programs in ESL.

TESOL: Teaching English to Speakers of Other Languages – a term that is used to distinguish English language teaching as a professional activity that requires specialized training. Also refers to the teacher examinations developed by Trinity College London (Cert. T ESOL and LTCL. Dip. TESOL).

TESOL: US-based international association of teachers of English as a second or foreign language. There are regional affiliates and many countries have their own affiliated associations.

Text: Any scripted or recorded production of a language presented to learners of that language. A text can be written or spoken and could be, for example, a poem, a newspaper article, a passage about pollution, a song, a film, an extract from a novel or a play, a passage written to exemplify the use of the past perfect, a recorded telephone conversation, a scripted dialogue or a speech by a politician. Total Physical Response

Method: Developed by Asher, where items are presented in the foreign language as 'orders', 'commands' and "instructions" requiring a physical response from the learner (e.g., 'opening a window' or 'standing up' after being asked, linguistically, to carry out such command).

Transactional tasks: These tasks are primarily concerned with the transfer of information: See interactional tasks.

Transfer: Knowledge of the L1 is used to help in learning the L2. Transfer can be positive, when the two language have similar structures, or it can be negative, when the two languages are different, and L1-induced errors occur. Trinity College London Responsible for the Certificate in TESOL and the Licentiate Diploma in TESOL examinations.

UCLES: University of Cambridge Local Examinations Syndicate. Syndicate of local examination centers around the world that administer the University of Cambridge ESOL examinations.

Universal grammar: A set of general principles that apply to all languages, rather than a set of particular rules.

Universal hypothesis: This states that certain universal linguistic properties determine the order in which the rules of a specific language are acquired. Thus, linguistic rather than cognitive factors determine acquisition.

University of Cambridge ESOL: Administered locally by UCLES. Is a British-based organization responsible for developing a number of important English language exams (including PET, FCE, CAE) and teacher training programs including the CELTA, CELTYL, and DELTA examinations.

Variability: Language learners vary in the use they make of their linguistic knowledge. This can be systematic or unsystematic.

Visa: An endorsement made by an authorized representative of one country upon a passport issued by another, permitting the passport holder entry into or transit through the country making the endorsement.

Workbook: A book which contains extra practice activities for learners to work on in their own time. Usually the book is designed so that learners can write in it and often there is an answer key provided in the back of the book to give feedback to the learners.

Yuan: Also known colloquially as a "kuai," is the base unit of present-day Chinese currency. Formally known as the Renminbi. (Chinese: 元; pinyin: *yuán*)

Bibliography

Agricultural Bank of China. *http://www.abchina.com/en/default.htm*

Asia for Educators. *http://afe.easia.columbia.edu/timelines/china_timeline.htm*

Bank of China. *http://www.boc.cn/en/*

China Construction Bank. *http://www.ccb.com/en/home/index.html*

China Foreign Teachers Union. *http://www.ChinaForeignTeachersUnion.org*

Chinese Ethnic Groups. *http://en.wikipedia.org/wiki/List_of_ethnic_groups_in_China*

Dale Carnegie's The 3 C's. *http://www.dalecarnegie.com/assets/1/7/Secrets_of_Success.pdf/*

Emoji and Dingbats. *http://unicode.org/faq/emoji_dingbats.html*

Emotional Intelligence. *http://en.wikipedia.org/wiki/Emotional_intelligence*

General TESOL Terminology. *http://quizlet.com/19305892/tesol-terminology-flash-cards/*

Gold, Thomas, Douglas Guthrie, and David Wank. 2002. *Social Connections in China: Institutions, Culture and the Changing Nature of Guanxi.* Cambridge: Cambridge University Press.

Graddol, David. 2006. English Next. British Council. *http://www.britishcouncil.org/learning-research-english-next.pdf*

IES Abroad. *http://www.iesabroad.org*

Industrial and Commercial Bank of China. *http://www.icbc.com.cn/ICBC/sy/default.htm*

It's time for messaging apps to quit the bullshit numbers and tell us how many users are active. techinasia.com. January 23, 2014. Steven Millward.

Kemp, Simon (2016, January). 2016 Digital Yearbook: *We Are Social's compendium of key digital statistics and data points for 232 countries around the world,* We Are Social. Retrieved from http://bit.ly/DSM2016YB

Kemp, Simon (2015, August). Digital Statshot China: *Key statistical indicators for Internet, mobile, and social media usage in China in August 2015,* We Are Social. Retrieved from http://bit.ly/DSM2016DI

Luo Xiwen, tr. *Bencao Gangmu: Compendium of Materia Medica.* 6 vols. Foreign Languages Press. 2003. ISBN 7-119-03260-7. (Review, Edward B. Jelks)

Maslow, A. H. (1943). A theory of human motivation. *Psychological Review* 50 (4) 370-96. Retrieved from *http://psychclassics.yorku.ca/Maslow/motivation.htm*

Ministry of Education of the People's Republic of China. *http://www.moe.edu.cn/*

Modern Chinese society. *http://www.nationsonline.org/oneworld/china.htm*

Money and Banking Terms. *http://www.dummies.com/how-to/content/money-and-banking-phrases-in-chinese.html*

Nishar, Deep (January 9, 2013). 200 Million Members! *LinkedIn Blog*. LinkedIn. Archived from the original on June 3, 2013.

Obama touts new China visa deal as way to create U.S. jobs, USA Today, November 10, 2014. *http://www.usatoday.com/story/ news/world/2014/11/10/apec-beijing-obama/18786007/*.

Ostrowski, Pierre; Gwen Penner (2009). *It's all Chinese to Me: an overview of culture & etiquette in China*. Tuttle. pp. 48–49. ISBN 978-0-8048-4079-8.

Passports and Visas. *http://www.passportsandvisas.com/visas/ visafaq.asp*

Relationship management. Retrieved from *http:// www.investopedia.com/terms/r/relationship-management.asp*

Tencent - Investor Relations - Financial Releases - 2014. Tencent. 2014-08-14.

Tencent Announces 2012 Fourth Quarter and Annual Results. PR Newswire. 2013-03-20.

Timeline of Chinese Dynasties and Other Key Events. Prepared by Michael Tsin, previously assistant professor of Chinese history, Columbia University; currently associate professor of Chinese history, University of North Carolina at Chapel Hill. Text ©1995 Columbia University, Asia in Western and World History: A Guide for Teaching, (Ainslie Embree and Carol Gluck, eds., Armonk, NY: M.E. Sharp Inc. 1995).

Types of Visas. Embassy of the People's Republic of China in the United States of America. *http://www.china-embassy.org/ eng/visas/hrsq/t1071018.htm*

United States Department of State, Bureau of Consular Affairs, US Visas. *http://travel.state.gov/content/visas/english/ general/americans-traveling-abroad.html*

Unschuld, Paul U. *Medicine in China: A History of Pharmaceutics*. University of California Press. 1986. ISBN 0-520-05025-8.

Von Rosen, Viveka (2012). *LinkedIn Marketing An Hour A Day*. Indianapolis, Indiana: John Wiley & Sons Inc. p. 2. ISBN 9781118358702.

Weixin (微信) – Tencent's Bringing the Mobile IM Revolution to the Mainstream. TechRice. September 21, 2011.

Williams, Dai (1999, April). Transitions: managing personal and organisational change. Retrieved from *http://www.eoslifework.co.uk/transmgt1.htm*

李时珍 (*Lǐ Shízhēn*) Biography. Retrieved from *http://bit.ly/1Nl8p6Q*

Index

A Briggs Passport & Visa Expeditors, 74
Academic/University, 27
Afghanistan, 37, 38
Agricultural Bank of China, 115, 119, 192
Angela's ESL Café, 92
Anhui, 32
Apple Watch, 139
APEC, 69
APPS, 140-143
Articulation agreements, 13, 152
AT&T, 112
ATM/Debit Cards, 117
    Discover, 117
    MasterCard, 75, 117
    UnionPay, 117
    Visa, 117
Australia, 47-49, 171

Bank of China, 115-116
Basic Requirements, 21
Beijing, 33-34, 44, 69, 93-94, 103, 122, 131, 136-138, 154
Bencao gangmu, 133-134
Bhutan, 37-38
Big 3, 111
Blackboard, 97
Boots, 75
British Council, 16, 92
Buck, 118
Burger King, 137-138
Burma, 37
Business Cards, 33, 160
Business Relationship(s), 159, 161
Business/Professional, 158

CALL, 106
Canada, 47-49, 92
Cantonese, 32
Career Path Opportunities, 15, 28
Carrefour, 136
Cash On-hand, 132

CDMA, 112-113
CEFR, 28
CELTA, 21, 28
Central Government, 150
CET-4, 19
CET-6, 19
CFTU, 86, 93
Children, 18, 27, 41-42, 46, 62, 167
China Construction Bank, 115, 119, 142
China Foreign Teachers Union, 86, 93
China Mobile, 111, 113
China Telecom, 111, 113
China Unicom, 111, 113
China Visa Service Center, 74
Chinese and Asian Acculturation, 139
Chinese Apartments, 126, 128
Chinese Cuisine Styles, 31
Chinese Currency, 40, 118, 121
Chinese Diet, 31, 133
Chinese Dynasties, 31-32, 170
Chinese Education, 41
Chinese Embassy, 54, 56, 58, 69, 73, 75-76, 84-85
Chinese Flag (wu xing hong qu), 39
Chinese Gift-giving, 34
Chinese Government, 63, 68, 113, 115
Chinese Grocery Stores, 135
Chinese Identification Card, 95
Chinese Law, 78, 87
Chinese Medical Journal, 133
Chinese Recruiters, 87, 95
Chinese Relationships, 147
Chinese Students, 41-42, 45, 96-98, 102, 147, 163
Chinese University System, 12
Chongqing, 40, 133, 136
Chopsticks, 35, 100, 126-127

Classroom Dynamics, 163
Classroom Language, 104
Classroom Management, 24, 41, 44-45, 90, 96-97, 163-165
Coaching Skills, 90
Commercial Activity, 59
Common European Framework of Reference for Languages, 28
Communist Party of China, 44
Comprehension, 17-18, 20
Connections, 26, 91, 161
Contract(s), 76-82, 86-87, 93, 118-119, 130-132, 164, 166
    Contract Anatomy, 77, 80
    Contract Fundamentals, 77
    Contract Scams, 77, 86
    Contractual Agreement, 80, 82, 120
    Contractual Period, 77-78, 80
    Length of Contract, 87
    Liquidated Damages, 81
    Termination Clause, 81
Counterfeit money, 118
Cover Letter, 89
CPC, 44
Critical Reasoning, 18-19
Cultivate Relationships, 162
Cultural Relationships, 34
Cultural Transition, 37, 139-141
Curriculum, 143, 145, 162
Curriculum Development, 46, 148, 150, 165
CVS, 75
Cycle of Favors, 162

Dale Carnegie, 90
    Three C's, 90
Dave's ESL Café, 92

Dean, 88
DELTA, 28
Deputy Director, 88, 149
Desired Qualifications, 21
Dico's, 137-138
Director of Studies (DOS), 106
Disney English, 46, 220
Disruptive Students, 97

EAP, 106-107
Eastern Zhou, 32
Eastern/Later Han, 32
Ebola, 22
Educational Reform, 40
EF English First, 46
Electrical Outlets, 128
ELL, 106-107
Emoji, 139, 143-144
Emotional Intelligence, 22-23
EMT, 106
English Corner, 98, 100
English, International Language, 14-16
English Teaching Jobs, 148
ESOL, 108
ESP, 106
Essential APPs Categories, 140-143
    Connectivity, 143
    Finance/Valuation, 142
    Metros/Subways, 142
    Social media, 142
    Teaching, 142
    Travel, 143
Evaluations, 96, 101
Extracurricular activities, 11, 43, 96, 99, 165

Face *(Chinese culture)*, 24, 97
Facebook, 86, 95, 114
Faculty, 150, 152
Family reunion, 52, 60
Fast Food Restaurants, 133, 137-138
Finance, 27, 115
First Impressions, 96
Flickr, 114
FLTRP Cup English
  Public Speaking Contest, 100
Food Familiarity, 136
Foreign Affairs Officer, 91
Foreign Currency, 116, 122
Foreign-Exchange Transactions, 116
Foreign Experts, 12, 44, 67, 87
Foreign Guest(s), 79, 91, 93
Foreign University, 151
Foreigner, 21-23, 35, 49, 52-53, 56, 58, 62-63, 65-68, 100, 126, 129
Foreigner Price, 126
Foster Care, 52, 61-62
Friendship, 11, 35, 100, 162
Fruits and Vegetables, 135
Fujian, 32

Gao Kao, 19, 167
Gift-Giving (also see *Chinese Gift-Giving*), 34
Global Culture, 143
Gmail, 114
Gold Star TEFL, 92
Good Health, 21-22
Google Plus, 114
Government-Run Schools, 12, 45-46
Grammar, 17-18, 45
Great Firewall, 113

Great Internet Wall of China, 111, 113
Great Wall of China, 111, 113
GSM, 112-113
Guangzhou, 103, 122, 131
Guanxi, 26, 153, 161-163
Guanxi vs. Networking, 161
Guided Mandarin, 104

Haggling, 128
Han Dynasty, 32
HIV, 22
Hong Kong, 7, 11, 43, 114, 122, 129, 136-137
Housing, 46, 77-79, 87, 110, 116, 124-125, 127, 129, 131, 164, 166
Human Motivation, 36
Hunan, 32

Idiomatic Expressions, 18, 104-105
  To kill two birds with one stone, 105
  When in Rome, do as the Romans, 23, 105
IELTS, 28-29, 167
IEP, 108
India, 37-38
Industrial and Commercial Bank of China, 115-116, 142
Industry Terminology, 106
Information Department of the
  Ministry of Foreign Affairs of China, 57
Instant Messaging, 154
Intangible Qualifications, 15, 22-23
International Affairs Office, 149
International Schools, 45-46

International University Relations, 142, 146
Intimate Component, Relationships, 162
Invitation Letter, 56, 58-60, 62-63, 65, 67-68, 76, 84-85
Invoice/Receipt (fa piao), 132
iPhone 6S, 139

Japan, 11, 143
Japanese, 34, 143
Jiangsu, 32
Junior Achievement, 89

Kazakhstan, 37-138
KFC, 137-138
Kuai, 118, 123
Kyrgyzstan, 37-38

L1, 18-19, 106
L2, 17, 107
Language Acquisition Focus Areas, 15-16, 18-20
Laos, 7, 37-38
Leasing, 124
    Leasing Agent Commission, 132
    Leasing Agents, 124
    Leasing Agents, responsibility of, 125
    Leasing Agreements, 129
    Leasing Amounts, 131
    Leasing Deposit, 131
LEP, 106, 108
Lesson Plan, 98-99, 165
Letters of Reference, 96, 101

Li Shizhen (李时珍), 133
LinkedIn, 142, 154, 158-159
List of Sensitive Topics and Keywords, 114
Listening, 17-19, 97-98, 160
Local Language, 35, 139
Local Police Department, 132
Local Price, 126
London Drugs, 75

Macau, 43, 114, 129
Mainland Banking and Finance, 110, 115
Major Chinese Financial Institutions, 115-116
Major Provincial Universities, 150
Mandarin, 18, 35, 37, 39, 80, 87, 95, 104-105
Maslow's Hierarchy of Needs, 36
McDonald's, 137-138
Medical, 22-23, 27, 77, 87, 133, 167
Memorandum of Understanding, 152
Meten English, 46
METRO *(grocery store),* 136
Mi4, 139
Mianzi, 24
Middle Kingdom, 9-10, 30
MIIT, 113
Ming Dynasty, 33, 133
Ministry of Education, 40-41, 43-44, 148-149
Ministry of Industry
    and Information Technology, 113
Mobile phone usage, 139
Mobile Subscriber, 139-140

Modern Chinese Society, 30, 33
Mongolia, 37-38
Muslim Dishes, 135
Myanmar, 37-38

National People's Congress, 39
Neighboring Countries, 30, 37
Nepal, 30, 37
Networking, 26, 153, 160-163
New Oriental, 46
New Zealand, 47-49
Non-Native English Speaker, 25-26
Non-White English Speaker, 15, 24
North Central Xi'an, 135
North Korea, 37-38

Open Markets, 135
Oxford Seminars, 92

Pakistan, 37-38
Papa John's Pizza, 138
Passport, 21, 47-48, 50, 54-55, 61, 63-65, 69-70, 72, 74-76, 80, 82, 119-120, 132
Pebble Smartwatch, 139
Peking University, 150
People's Republic of China, 33, 39-40, 43, 69, 75, 80, 83
People's Republic of China President Xi Jinping, 69
Personal Relationships, 22, 151
Personal Space, 34
Pizza Hut, 138
Policy Changes, 149
Political or Religious Discussions, 91

Public Service Bureau, 44, 80-81, 87
Public Toilets, 37
Puer Tea, 135
Putonghua, 16, 35, 40

Qin (Ch'in) Dynasty, 32
QQ, 89, 120, 141-145, 151, 154-157
Quanjude, 138

Reading, 12, 17, 19, 45
Reciprocal obligations, 162
Recruiter, 26, 29, 86-89, 93-95, 101, 103, 149
RED STAMP, 82, 130
Relationship Management, 7, 153, 159
Relationships, 22-23, 34, 91, 93, 146-147, 151, 159-162
Renminbi, 40, 116, 118
Rental Amounts, 130
Residence Permit, 23, 50, 60-66, 68, 77-78, 94
Rite-Aid, 75
RSA, 108
Rural China, 19-20, 140
Russia, 11, 37-38

SAFEA, 41, 44, 77
SAIC License Number, 95
Sample Interview Questions, 153, 163
   Classroom management, 165
   Relocation/Housing, 166
   Salary, 166
   Teaching Position, 164
   Training and Development, 165

SAMS, 136, 139
Samsung Galaxy, 139
Schedule of payment, 130
School of Foreign Languages, 88
School of International Affairs, 88
Search for housing, 124-125
Sending money, 115, 119
Serious Teachers, 92
Shandong, 32
Shane English, 46
Shang Dynasty, 32
Shanghai, 44, 103, 122, 131, 136-137
Shenzhen, 44, 103, 122, 131, 136
SIM Cards, 111-112
Skype, 143, 151
Smart Devices, 114, 139-140, 143-144
Social Behavior, 34
Social Media, 19, 97, 114, 139, 141-143, 145, 154, 160
Song Dynasty, 31
South Africa, 12, 47-49
Southwestern Yunnan, 135
Speaking, 15, 17-20, 48-49, 90, 97-100, 104, 107, 120, 125, 148, 158, 167
Specialty Shops, 133, 137
Sports Competition, 100
Spring Festival, 33
Sprint, 112
Standard Apartment, 78
Starbucks, 137
State Administration of Foreign Expert Affairs, 41, 44, 77
STDs, 22
Student Exchange, 150, 152
Student-Teacher Relationship, 99
Subway *(restaurant)*, 138

Supporting Documents, Visa, 54, 56
  C Visa, 56
  D Visa, 56
  F Visa, 56
  G Visa, 57
  J1 Visa, 57
  J2 Visa, 58
  L Visa, 58
  M Visa, 59
  Q1 Visa, 60
  Q2 Visa, 62
  R Visa, 63
  S1 Visa, 63
  S2 Visa, 65
  X1 Visa, 66
  X2 Visa, 67
  Z Visa, 67
Szechuan, 32

Taiwan, 11, 34, 43, 91, 114, 129
Tajikistan, 37-38
TCM, 133-134
Teacher Salaries, 103
Teaching Acronyms, 104-105
Teaching Credentials, 167
Teaching English to Speakers of Other Languages, 28, 108
Teaching Specialties, 15, 27
Teaching Style, 28, 90, 101
Technical, 27, 44
TEFL, 21, 28, 92, 107-108
Telecommunications, 111
TEM-4, 19
TEM-6, 19
TESL, 92, 108

TESOL, 15, 21, 25, 27-29, 41, 44-45, 77-78, 80, 86-88, 90, 92-93, 96-99, 101-109, 114, 116, 118-120, 130, 141, 148, 154, 157, 159, 163, 167-168
TESOL Blacklist, 88, 93
TESOL International (US), 92
The Big Four, 116
The Dynasties Song, 32
Tibet, 34, 91
Timeline of Chinese Dynasties, 32
T-Mobile, 112
To save face, 24
TOEFL, 109
Town & Village Enterprises (TVEs), 116
Traditional Chinese Medicine, 133
Translator, 139, 152
Travel visa, 48, 94
Twitter, 114, 157
Types of Certifications, 15, 27

UCLES, 109
United Kingdom, 16, 47-49
United States, 16, 30, 39, 47-49, 70, 74, 91, 112
Universal adapter, 129
University of Toledo, 150
US Citizens, 34, 48-49, 70-71, 74, 112
US Department of State's Bureau of Consular Affairs, 49
US Dollar, 118
US President Barack Obama, 69

Vanguard *(grocery store)*, 136
Verizon, 112

Vietnam, 37-38
Virtual Private Network, 111, 114
Visa Application for Study in China, 66
Visa Application Form, 50, 54, 72, 75
Visa Categories, 38-41
  C Visa, 56
  D Visa, 56
  F Visa, 56
  G Visa, 56
  J1 Visa, 56
  J2 Visa, 56
  L Visa, 56
  M Visa, 56
  Q1 Visa, 57
  Q2 Visa, 57
  R Visa, 57
  S1 Visa, 57
  S2 Visa, 58
  X1 Visa, 58
  X2 Visa, 58
  Z Visa, 58
Visa Fee Structure, 47, 74
Visa *(travel)*, 48, 94
  10-Year Chinese Visa, 47, 70
Visual Personal Space, 34
Vocabulary, 17, 19, 104
VPN, 114
VPN *block list*, 114

Walgreens, 75
Wall Street English, 46
Walmart, 75, 136
We Are Social, 154
WeChat, 89, 120, 141-145, 154, 157
Western financial institutions, 116-117
Western grocery stores, 133, 136

Western networking 162
Western Social Media, 114
Western Union, 115, 119
Western Zhou, 32
Western/Former Han, 32
WIN-WIN, 94, 150
Wiring Money, 115, 119
Work Permit, 23, 44, 50, 76, 84
Writing, 17, 20, 45, 89, 97, 103

Xi'an Jiaotong University, 150
Xia (Hsia) Dynasty, 32
Xiaomi, 139
Xinjiang, 34, 91
Yangtze, 40
Yellow, 40
YouTube, 114
Yuan, 33, 40, 115, 118, 120-123
Yuan Anatomy 115, 118
Yunnan Minzu University, 150
Yunnan Normal University, 145

Zhejiang, 1832
Zhen Kungfu, 138
Zhong xi wen hua jiao hui, 163
Zhou (Chou) Dynasty, 32
Z-visa, 22, 44, 49-50, 67, 94, 166

The conversation continues at:

- Study abroad resources
- China travel
- Updates in today's Chinese society
- See what's happening in China TESOL
- Respond to our blog posts and comments
- Provide us with updates in China TESOL
- Share your thoughts—get involved!

Connect with us via social media

www.ingramcontent.com/pod-product-compliance
Lightning Source LLC
Chambersburg PA
CBHW051119160426
43195CB00014B/2268